A Gift From the Grave

Dearest Lady Golfer,

Goes great with a
few glasses of wine.

Hope you enjoy.

yours,
Swami

A Gift From the Grave

✦

an incredible true story

Brent (swami) Bittner

iUniverse, Inc.

New York Bloomington Shanghai

A Gift From the Grave
an incredible true story

iUniverse books may be ordered through booksellers or by contacting:

iUniverse
1663 Liberty Drive
Bloomington, IN 47403
www.iuniverse.com
1-800-Authors (1-800-288-4677)

ISBN: 978-0-595-46777-8 (pbk)
ISBN: 978-0-595-70507-8 (cloth)
ISBN: 978-0-595-91069-4 (ebk)

Printed in the United States of America

Contents

Foreword

"A Gift From The Grave" is a true story written for you, my son Keenan. This is my gift for you on your thirteenth birthday. My old man gave me a bottle of beer on a hot July afternoon for my thirteenth birthday. It was good. Instead of giving you a beer Keenan, I will give you this book. I hope that you find it interesting and the father-son parables rewarding. To hell with hope kid, you are going to laugh your head off.

The names of a few individuals in this book have been changed for reasons of privacy. Great effort has been made to ensure that the dialogue quoted is as exact as to what was actually said. Late night dialogue may be a bit off due to drinking, yet the thrust of the message conveyed is true. Messages are in people and not in words.

This book is about a trip to magical India. It is about Creation, love for our Creator and appreciation of the energy in the universe. It is also about the love that completes the father-son bond.

There is a wake for my father. His death leaves me wiser; confirming and enriching my spirituality. Many messages result for Keenan, my wonderful listening son.

This is a guy book for real men. It may not be for some quiche nibbling Perrier sipping wussy, however, the true story in itself will give goose bumps to even the most hoity-toity of all.

The author does not apologize for any grammatical errors in this book. Ever since his grade five teacher pulled him out of his desk by his hair, for not writing a sentence correctly, he has had a distaste for using <u>proper</u> English. Furthermore, do not expect the author to write like an editor who has a thesaurus implanted beside his hypothalamus. I am here to relay a funny and interesting story that even a thirteen year old can comprehend.

If you do not appreciate the style and content of this true story you can just go … No, I cannot say that. My mother may end up putting down her Harlequin Romance novel and actually read this.

Joy to the world, brothers and sisters!

Love swami

Leaving for India

It is a sunny afternoon as Kavi and I sit in a Boeing 757 on the tarmac at the Edmonton International Airport. Kavi is the Indian name for my great and best friend Peter George. Kavi was born in Southern India and came to Canada when he was seven years old. He is engaged to an Indian woman named Phanni, in his home state of Kerala, at the end of December. He was introduced to her through a relative. He flew to meet her for the first time in the United Arab Emirates back in March of this year. Both of us are very excited.

This trip will turn out to be the most important journey in my life. I have heard and read many stories about magical India. Almost all of the world religions have roots there. There is strong evidence that shows that the first civilizations on earth were in the Hindus Valley. Some say Jesus hung out in India during his twenties. You have to be a dumb ass not to be intrigued with India.

"Do you remember what I have told you about being safe when traveling in India?" Kavi asks.

"What part of being safe?" I reply, "using a money belt or not letting a stranger become my tour guide?"

"That is good. Did you bring toilet paper?"

"Yes. Three rolls."

"That is it?"

"Yes. I am going to learn how to use the water like an Indian. I already know which hand to use."

Kavi chuckles and says, "Make sure you use your right hand when you are eating. You do not want to mix it up at the wedding dinner. There will be over five hundred people there and you will likely be the only white person. Eyes will be on you."

"Thanks Kavi. I will not let you down."

Kavi advises, "We have a two hour stop in Los Angeles. We have to collect our luggage after landing and check in with Malaysian Airlines. Once that is done we can relax with a couple of beers. If you are lucky we may be able to find you a smoking room."

"Thank you for your understanding Kavi. I brought some nicotine gum and tried a piece but it tastes awful and it seems to stab at my stomach walls."

All goes well with the luggage transfer and we find a stand up bar. We are smiling and giggling like two schoolboys catching a glimpse of the pretty girls panties. We have two beers each and ask for the tab. The smile leaves my face.

"Excuse me Sir." I call out to the bartender. "Is this correct? Twenty-six dollars for four beers. I do not mind paying for beer but this seems a little excessive. Furthermore, they are not even real beer. They are weak."

"You must be a Canadian who is used to the stronger beer," he replies with a grin, "keep in mind that you are in an airport."

"I understand. Thank you Sir." That is the way it goes in most airports. They try to bend you over and take you for all its worth.

Walking away I ask Kavi, "So, how did I do?"

"Not bad. But in India you will need to be more assertive and develop your Indian accent. Practice by saying, *"GO TO THE TEMPLE AND SAY YOUR PRAYERS."*

I try. *"GO TO THE TEMPLE AND SAY YOUR PRAYERS."*

"Not bad. You need to be more rhythmical. Your voice needs to flow. Accentuate the 'ple' in temple. Remember 'Apu' in the *Simpsons*. Do it like that."

"How is this Kavi? *GO TO THE TEMPLE AND SAY YOUR PRAYERS!"*

"Good. You're getting better. Let's find a bathroom and a smoke room before we board."

"WHAT THE HELL. GOOD IDEA KAVI. LET'S GO TO THE TEMPLE AND SAY OUR PRAYERS." We are laughing so hard in the line up to go through the security screening, other passengers are looking at us strangely.

Holy Lick! This stubble jumper has never seen the inside of a plane so big. It has two aisles and holds many passengers. A couple of the Malaysian Airline stewardesses are gorgeous. They are wearing bright blue flower pattern Kimono's with pink trim. One lady is of mixed race. Kavi figures that she is of Malaysian, Indian and European descent. Her smile is enticing. This is a classy airline with classy stewardesses.

We are flying over what seems like islands. There are hundreds of them with specks of light scattered about. I try to figure out where we are and the most likely flight path by making a mental map of the Pacific Ocean and Asia. It is the middle of the night. Everyone else is asleep on the plane. It is eerie and quite weird. Except for the jet softly flying at forty thousand feet, without a hint of turbulence, everything else is tombstone still. I am a little concerned of not knowing where we are as I have never flown across the ocean before. I look out the window and now only see darkness below. I am suddenly reminded of him, the bloody devil, Beelzebub, Cloven Hoof, Red Face, Prince of Darkness, Yama, Lord of Death, Satan. The guy who I call The Big Bastard.

I first met The Big Bastard when I was four years old. Some may argue that he came by as a result of a turbulent and troubled family life. Dad drank, yelled a lot and beat me some. Don't get me wrong, he never punched me with a closed fist. Just slapped me around some, not bruising me or anything. He would whack me across the head really hard with an open hand or kick me in the ass hard. At times it seemed like a whipping boy type of thing enhanced by a quick and mean temper. I remember once being thrown against the kitchen wall and landing upside down on my head. I never forgot to wear rubber boots when told to after that one. I was afraid of Dad. He was no Satan though. Dad would have shit his pants if he came face to face with a ghoul or evil spirit. Fred Leo Bittner was no match for The Big Bastard. I suspect that Dad had his own demons to deal with though on top of trying to provide for six kids. It could be that The Big Bastard is a psychological manifestation of my father. I doubt that this is the case. I believe The Big Bastard is a representation of evilness in the world while I am the opposite. Father was not evil, just mixed up and misguided at times.

The Big Bastard always came by to visit in the same manner. You know when the television is not on a channel; no cable, just a loud fuzzy sound. Loud static, Shhhhhhhhhhhhhhhhhhhhhhhhhh. I'm ready to fall asleep, right on the edge; that short period between consciousness and sub-consciousness. I know I'm not asleep because I try to make the whole scene go away by imagining the face of Jesus in between a square section in the slatted thin metal bunk bed frame three and a half feet above my face. The buzz sound comes, the ceiling opens up and The Big Bastard drops down. The room is suddenly enlarged. I'm frozen stiff. There he is, all thirty feet of him, levitating upright fifteen feet off the ground. Grinning, then sneering, he does not say a thing. Didn't have to. I know who he is. He'd hang around for a while. Scaring the be Jesus out of me. Twenty or thirty minutes later I come out of it.

As a kid, I felt that The Big Bastard was after my soul. Sometimes The Big Bastard would pay me a visit in the middle of the day. I'd be laying on the living room floor on a late Saturday afternoon, after completing my weekend chores, in front of my folks while they'd be watching television. Must have nodded off for a minute or two. Television was quite boring when I was a kid, except for the cartoons. We only had one channel in Melville, Saskatchewan back then. Well, I was lying there and The Big Bastard comes. Before you know it, my supine body was jumping around like a single piece of sizzling bacon in an open extremely hot frying pan—convulsing like crazy. Mom said later that I was off the bloody floor. She figured the devil was in me. When I heard that, I wondered if the devil was pissed off because he did not get to take a shot at me or my soul when I nearly died a year earlier. Anyway, she was definitely wrong about him being in me. He was either trying to get in me or simply trying to get at me. Perhaps it was simple intimidation for some future event.

The Big Bastard would visit me a lot and try to get in me, but I would never let him in despite being petrified motionless. I may have physically been a little prick, but I was strong inside. In my childhood, you had to be. Thank God that my poor mother took me to Sunday School and introduced me to Jesus. To me Jesus was superhuman and a friend whom I could talk to any time. Just like I could talk to our Creator at any time. Never had a visit from Jesus though. He doesn't visit as He does not have to. I visit Him and God in my head and heart.

I estimate that The Big Bastard has come around more than two hundred times in my life. I can't say for certain, but I believe he was there simply to scare the shit out of me and show me what evil really is. That he is the king of evil and he rules. He wasn't there to invite me to join him like when Darth Vader tries to recruit Luke Skywalker. Even when I think of it today it seems that he was there to let me know he was real and in the neighborhood. It wasn't really fair back then. A big bloody thirty-foot dude, little stumps on his forehead and all, scaring the shit out of a little boy.

The Big Bastard has very little visible body hair except for a short black goatee and thin dark eyebrows. The kind of goatee that has hair growing only on the end of the chin coming to a sharp point an inch and a half in length. He is bare-chested showing off his upper body muscles covered with light red skin. His face is a brighter red than the rest of his skin, like a crimson blood red. He has a chiseled chin and a broad forehead. He has wrinkles on his forehead of a fifty year old man. He eyes are dark and difficult to read. Thinking about them just now, they remind me of Charles Manson, absent dark eyes, hollow and devoid of any life. The Big Bastard wears ugly brown pants when he visits. His slacks are well worn and tattered at the ends. You would think he would dress better, then again, this may be his fighting outfit. The Big Bastard is in shape. He has the build of a gymnast.

Every time; television buzz sound, the ceiling opens and The Big Bastard drops in. I am always alone in the enlarged room after he drops in, except once. Shhhhhhhhhhhhhhhhhhhhhhhhh.

The room suddenly expands to about sixty by sixty feet square and the ceiling about the same height. It has cream walls. Mom and Dad are in the enlarged room with me. We are crouched behind a couch. Dad whispers to me to be quiet. Mom puts her index finger to her mouth motioning me to be quiet. We all know why. He is close by. The loud eerie buzz sound sounds again and The Big Bastard drops in. Mom and Dad stay quiet and leave the room while I am frozen shitless, with The Big Bastard staring me down. When I come to I am all sweaty and panting, scared to death again, not wanting to fall asleep.

That's how I know that The Big Bastard is not some sort of psychological representation of my father. The Big Bastard had scared him right beside me. Both Mom and Dad knew who he was and knew to be quiet before The Big Bastard drops through the ceiling. I think that it has already been said that my old man was tough but he was not even one thousandth as tough or scary as The Big Bastard.

The events became so intense that my mother would comment, "If this keeps up, I am going to have to take you to a shrink." It scared her to see her son laying down on the area rug, watching television in front of her and see me twist around and come off the floor like frying bacon. Mom told me that it was as if someone was shoving me on a bed and bouncing me up and down with great force with my limbs flailing about. In my mind I was simply in a frozen state. Trying to wake myself up did not work. Mother thought that I could have been possessed. She did not know it was The Big Bastard who was doing this to me. I did not want to tell her either. There was no way that I wanted him to pay her a visit. Besides, my mother had enough on her plate already. God love her.

Funny thing is, all this started well before I went to kindergarten, before I had ever seen any depiction of Satan in a book, movie or the like. I may have seen his head on a can of Devilled Ham but that would have seemed to be a cartoon character to me. *Speaking of cartoon characters, Keenan did you know that my first word was Nahbob? Yes, Nahbob. I picked it up by watching the Nabob coffee commercials before I could walk. Mom loves telling the story of me being in the playpen in front of the television squatting and jumping up and down repeatedly when the commercial came on. Mom says that I was nine or ten months old.*

Not that impressive, though, just a little bit funny. Usually a child's first word is "mommy" or "daddy", not a brand. What is impressive is that I had you saying "characterization" before you were two years old. You may not remember it but I talked to you from the get go like a man. No sissy talk from me. Man talk. Tough talk. I said no like "NO" and you listened. You grew up to be so damn respectful, polite and well mannered. Terrible twos? Hah! That is the result of poor parenting. Sometimes it could be unfortunate biology. You walk into any Wal-mart and I will find you a dozen mothers that really should not have procreated. What strikes most people about you is your way with words. You have a gifted vocabulary and know when and how to use it. That makes me proud.

I capitalize The Big Bastard because to me he is a real representation of what is evil. You can call him Satan but I cannot scientifically prove that The Big Bastard is Satan. Nor can I absolutely prove to the world that he is a demon and buddy of Satan. What is important is that I show that I perceived The Big Bastard and felt his negative energy. One cannot deny that there is evil amongst us. A man who kills his wife must be struck with evil. Charles Manson is definitely evil. Hitler, deranged like Manson but also just plain evil. Each and every pedophile, past, present and future is evil. Anyone who rapes is evil.

Of course evilness is a matter of characterization that can be defined over a broad spectrum. From super evil like The Big Bastard or Satan, next to guys like Manson and Hitler, then to white collar criminals, and then to quasi-evil at the smaller end of the spectrum where the wife-beaters, thieves and petty criminals sit.

Even a woman who uses her sexuality to get what she wants materially has a touch of evilness. Where do you think the saying, which is not often said because most men do not have the balls to say it, "women are inherently evil" comes from? When I say this to a right-minded woman she agrees with me. She understands human nature on the female side. Look at Adam, Eve and that damn apple! Hee, hee. Do not take me wrong ladies, there is usually an exception to the rule or in this case, a sexist generalization.

The Big Bastard episodes are not simple nightmares, but much, much more. You know why? I have had some really groovy dreams and some pretty neat nightmares. From flying, being able to move and web like Spiderman (without the costume, damn it), to hanging out with friendly aliens on their ship over the ice rink at St. Henry's school in Melville.

These dreams occur in deep REM stuff. Not within minutes of when you are just entering sleep.

The Big Bastard does not strike with his fists or anything. He crushes your soul with fear; the fear of death and an eternity of suffering. He floats there sneering, freezes you so you cannot move a limb. You lay in a state of motionless anxiety, yet he makes you sweat and tremble. Crushes you with pressure so you cannot breathe. No words are mouthed. There is no passage of time with The Big Bastard towering over.

The Big Bastard only comes around just after I nod off, never in the middle or at the end of a nights sleep. He came a number of times after lunch at naptime just before watching the *Edge of Night* with Mom when I was five. He came mostly at night though. It became so bad when I was in grade school I wanted to die because I was so afraid of The Big Bastard. I would try to suffocate myself, with my face in the pillow, night after night. One night I took my mother's sleeping pills, about eight of them, that were left in a bottle in the bathroom medicine cabinet. I remember that I went to school as usual and slept at my grade three desk most of the day. Mrs. Taylor let me sleep. She knew and understood me and must have realized that something was wrong and just let me be. She was so sexy. I made her love cards that had pop ups in them when I was in grade two art class. She appreciated the one-sided romance. I would see more of her years later when I became her paperboy.

I know that I am alive today for the sole reason in that I have God on my side. God wants me to contribute to the cause because I know how to love and am not afraid to kick Satan's or The Big Bastard's ass. I cannot wait for the opportunity. I do not care if he comes by shooting fire-balls out of his ass. I will still pound the shit out of him. He has it coming.

Some people may think that I am either full of shit or some megalomaniac for saying this but they can kiss my behind. This is far beyond belief; this is personal knowledge. I will debate anyone in the world over this. Bring on any atheist, agnostic, what have you and I will kick their ass with words. One condition though. The loser would have to amputate their non-writing hand. *No fear Keenan as your father went to the national debates in grade twelve and had a party. Hey kid, I was already there and felt success-*

ful. Being one of the top guys from Saskatchewan was enough for me. Chasing women and drinking is a lot more fun than preparing for bogus debates on issues of no real importance—as long as you do it in moderation. Trouble is that the term 'moderation' varies in depth from person to person. Meanings are in people and not in words. Remember that Keenan, meanings are in people and not in words.

There are a couple of events that you should know about that may weigh in on your take of whether you think your father is nuts or true blue.

It is the third week in May. I am six years old. My parents left us five kids in the care of my oldest sister, Brenda, so they could go to a farm and buy some eggs. I am at Kinsmen Park, which is kitty corner from our house and directly West of Central School in Melville, Saskatchewan. There is a baseball game going on. I am with George Beddome, my buddy from across the back alley. We are on the top bench of some baseball bleachers that are about eight feet high. Mike Whihak is also there along with some spectators. I do not know if I am pushed or if I simply jump on my own free will. In any event, I land in a partially petrified rose bush. A branch as hard as stone punctures my side and makes a four inch gap in the front side of my left hip. It goes through my large intestine and penetrates another part of the intestine. I land and feel a great shock inside my body. I start bawling, big time. George Beddome and a baseball player help me. My sister Brenda says it was Dow Famulak. They have one of my arms over each of their shoulders and take me home. I look down while sitting against the old wooden garage door and see a gaping hole in my side just over the waist of my jeans. Blood soaked the left side of my pants. George runs across the alley to get his parents. My older sisters, Brenda, Dana and Karen are of course shocked by the sight. I ask them for a big band-aid to cover the hole. I am going into shock.

I remember being in Mr. Beddome's car laying across Laura Beddome's lap. She says that I am becoming as stiff as a board. She really cared for me. I remember waking up during the surgery and seeing metal claps, two doctors and a nurse. I was outside of my body looking down. I remember seeing the opening of the wound and the forceps in Dr. Millette's hands. Mother told me later that I was very close to dead and that I lost a third of my blood. She also said that while at the farm she had a premonition and needed to return home. She somehow knew that something bad happened to her son. A six-inch stick broke off inside and was embedded through my intestines. One doctor was going to just stitch up the hole. Dr. Millette shows up, takes over and smartly thinks that he should have a good look around deeper in my gut and cuts me open. It could be that The Big Bastard was taking a run at my soul. I doubt that was the case. More like a guardian angel or something like that, protecting me from death. Perhaps God needs me around to do more good. Dr. Millette finds and removes the stick, cleans out my gut and stitches me up. So I miss the last six weeks of school and have a great time—after I no longer needed a bedpan and could make it to the toilet on my own.

After I moved to Saskatoon, Saskatchewan, for college I get a job at the Saskatoon Arena, home of the Saskatoon Blades junior hockey team. I fit in well at the arena because I had experience being a rink rat at the Melville Arena, during in high school, driving the Zamboni, mopping floors and cleaning toilets. I needed the money for university and beer. My parents helped out as much as they could which I am thankful for. With such a large family they could only afford to pay about a fifth of the cost. For the most part I helped put myself through college working half time over a ten-year stint. It was great. *Enjoy being a student kid, as there is no life like it. Just be aware.*

One day in early March, Jim and I were vacuuming the heating ducts way up in the roof of the arena. I am the guy with the nozzle. Jim is working the vacuum and hose. The hose is more than forty feet long. We finished the east side of the arena over the last few days. It is a very big job as the main ducts are about six feet in diameter. We use a triple extension ladder to get up to the main duct and I climb on top. A thick layer of dust awaits me.

We move to the North end of the arena. Not thinking things through we decide to lean the ladder against a vent that is made of sheet metal and is about eight or ten feet long. It protrudes straight down from the main vent and has a semi-circular end vent where the heat exits. The idea is to get to the top of the ladder and vacuum the vent as we can see the dust from thirty feet below. The ladder is placed in the aisle between the seats. The Saskatoon Blades are having practice and some of the players are being interviewed by the local news media. I climb up, taking the nozzle with me while Jim feeds me the hose. I get to the top. Creak. Creak.

I yell down to Jim, "I don't think it is going to hold!"

"Let go of the nozzle! The vent is moving!"

I drop the hose but it is too late. Creak! Crunch! The vent breaks loose from it's base. I fall. Thank God that I hang onto the rungs of the ladder for dear life. I land on the ladder, which lands straight down the aisle. The ladder cushions the landing. The vent lands with an echoing crash behind me closer to the Plexiglas. Somewhat fortunate I fall with the ladder in an arc and not straight down like the vent. I lose my wind and am knocked out unconscious for a few minutes. I come to and see the trainer for the Blades shooing the camera crew away. I walk out of there with two long continuous bruises developing from my shoulders to my thighs. It was like someone painted two long symmetrical purple lines on my body from shoulder to thigh.

A couple days later the boss makes me assist him in reattaching the vent. Go figure.

I will have to tell you a bit more of The Big Bastard later Keenan. Let me leave you with this thought. I know for a fact, as true as the sunrise and the sunset, The Big Bastard is real in one form or another. However, like black and white, rain and fire, true and false, in life there is evil and there is love. I choose God, life and love. Some people say that you have never really lived unless you have nearly died. Maybe being close to death awakens a person and drives them to appreciate life more. The more you appreciate life the easier it is to understand. What does not kill you makes you stronger. A struggle presented is an opportunity to overcome.

In the depths of the night being stuck between a snoring Indian and a fat guy from Malaysia proves tiresome. I really need to urinate. Fat guy is blocking an easy exit so I hold it in to my detriment later. As we silently fly towards Malaysia, I have Keenan to think about and write to.

Sitting in a cramped seat does not allow sleep so I look out the window and try to figure out what the hell is down there. We must still be flying over islands. There are many islands between Los Angeles and Taipei. They could be the Hawaii Islands or we could be farther along and flying along the coast of Japan. I don't know. Time has escaped me. Even the beautiful stewardesses must be sleeping. There is nothing to be heard except for the hum of the jet engines and my best friend's intermittent snores.

After an uneventful refueling in Taipei, we close in on Kuala Lumpur. It is late morning and I have not slept. That's okay. The descent is fabulous as the sky is clear. There are many plantations seen below. Rubber trees lined up in rows and columns. It is a large thick lush symmetrical mass of green. There are no canola or wheat fields, no prairie bush either. There is jungle surrounding vast squares of plantations.

Jobe, Kavi's brother-in-law, is at the airport waiting for us. We have a nine-hour layover here. We collect our bags and see Jobe standing in the arrival waiting area. Jobe is tall and skinny with black short wavy hair. He has an accent that is remarkably different from your average Indian. He has a bit of a lisp that prevents the lovable Apu type rhythm. Jobe turns out to be one hell of a nice guy. He reminds me of V.J. Singh because of his teeth, eyes, skin tone and other similar attributes.

Kuala Lumpur is a very clean city. They do not have much crime, nor do I see any bums. Malaysia is tough on crime, big time. The pilot advised the passengers when descending that importing drugs is punishable by death. I bring this up with Jobe as we drive.

Jobe explains, "They hung two Australians a couple of years ago for trying to smuggle in a big bag of marijuana."

I say to Jobe, "for marijuana?! I hate to see what they do to people who try to bring in hard drugs like cocaine."

"They would hang them also. There is not much drug smuggling into this country because of the strict and harsh laws. It is a country where you must obey the law."

Like Kavi, Jobe is a slow mo, mellow, water off a ducks back kind of guy. Jobe is married to Pengal who is Kavi's older sister. She can become fired up quite easily. They both know how to dance along with the firecracker without igniting her. Pengal is pretty, in good shape and is a good strong woman. I would not want to piss her off again boy. Look out if you make a comment on who wears the pants in the family. Do not go there. Do not challenge the firecracker. She may not enjoy your sense of humor. She is, without a doubt, attractive thunder following a few verbal bolts. She is so tough-minded and strong I do not doubt that she, like most stubborn older sisters, used to fight her brother Kavi well.

Jobe and Pengal's home is nice and spacious. It is two stories high and shares a common wall with another condo. The best feature of their home is the toilet, the Indian bidet. Toilet paper is no longer required. There is a half-inch hose connected to a faucet on the wall to the left. The toilet is akin to your standard western toilet. With tiles on the floor and partially up the walls, you can really focus on cleaning yourself. I soon learn that it is more advantageous to take your pants and underwear right off if you use the hose, otherwise get the water pressure right the next time.

Kavi and I spend most of the afternoon drinking beer in the driveway and enjoying the warm sun. We decide to go for a walk through the neighborhood. The trees in the park are rich in variety. The flowers are bright red and their stems dainty. We walk on the grass. I have not seen grass like this. It is matted and thick. There are seven young men playing a volleyball type of game over a six foot net. The court surface is compacted sand. They do not use their hands or arms to volley the ball over the net. They kick the ball with their feet and receive the ball with their thighs or the sides of their legs. It is like 'hackysack' except the ball is quite different. The ball is hollow, hard and about eight inches in diameter. It is made of a dry hardened bamboo type material that is woven.

I go and join in. "*WHAT THE HELL ARE YOU DOING?*" asks Kavi. "*YOU ARE GOING TO GET YOURSELF ALL HOT AND SWEATY.*" He is correct so I only play for five minutes and fit in well.

It is late evening and the multitude of people in the Madras airport is mind-boggling. There are hundreds of people crowding each other and jostling for position. There are no ropes to cattle you through to the customs check like in the West. They treat their cattle here better. I take a picture of Kavi waving up to me from the middle of the crowd. He fits in. I sure the hell do not.

Outside the terminal in the parking lot, the smell in the air hits me with a profuse pounding of sulfur. Two minutes later, the odor leaves and I am breathing so clearly. I have an intense sense of belonging. Kavi's soon to be father-in-law has three of his friends in the car to greet us.

We check in to an overly expensive hotel previously booked for us. Someone must think we are loaded with cash. After we check in, I make an appointment with the bell-boy for the next day to take us to exchange cash and pick up a few things.

After dropping our luggage off in the room we waste no time and head down to the restaurant. Our beer arrives and we have a good cheer. The beer is cold with decent head. It is not at all flat like I was told it would be; snakes, beggars and flat beer. What a crock. Indian men like their beer cold and full of zip like all beer connoisseurs. The hotel restaurant we are in is small and plain. The two waiters are glad to serve us. Their English is broken and weak. They are successful in telling us to keep things low key because they should not be serving us beer so late. I smell a bit of bullshit but give them the benefit of the doubt.

Kavi and I drink beer and talk of India and the wedding.

"Thank you for coming buddy!" Kavi blurts out and stands up to give me a hug.

"I would not miss this for the world. It is a once in a lifetime opportunity."

It turns out so. To travel to a far away country so rich in culture, people, history, and after reading about India and learning her ways from Kavi's family proves to be invaluable.

Kavi continues, "I think that you will like India. You have to be careful though. Don't be so trusting of others. Hide your money and pay attention to prices. Due to the fact that you are white locals will think you have much money and will take advantage of you. Not all people; vendors and the odd con man."

"Thanks for the advice brother. I am open to anything you can tell me that will make my experience better. I also want to ensure that your wedding turns out great."

"It will be and thanks again for coming all this way."

I reply with, "*GO TO THE TEMPLE AND SAY YOUR PRAYERS. DO NOT TRY TO CHEAT THE WHITE MAN SIR.*"

We clank our glasses and make cheers again. A beautiful French woman once said that saying "cheers" and clanking your glasses originated with the royals and aristocrats. Back then kings and queens, as well as people of influence, often killed their spouse for one reason or another. They were afraid of poison being slipped into their wines so they would clank their pewter glass hard enough and the wine would spill from glass to glass. The couple would look each other in the eyes and watch their partner drink. When that happened you knew you were safe.

"Let's have one more round and then I need to call it quits." Kavi says.

I give Kavi a sad look and say, "We need to be good to the boys so I can get some more beers to take up to the room."

"Don't go too crazy, you have to fly out tomorrow."

"No problem buddy. I will only get three. I am far too fired up to go to sleep."

"I will get them for you."

Kavi will be staying in here for a few days and I am to go meet his father, Nogandichen, in Cochin before traveling to Kavi's Uncle George's house. Madras is on the Eastern coast of India and Cochin is on the Western side but more South.

I open the window all the way, which allows me to get onto the ledge and sit comfortably. Kavi does not blink an eye as he is a heavy sleeper. I am straddling the window ledge lengthwise overlooking the once busy street below, drinking the first take home beer and smoking a cigarette, analyzing everything I see below. A security guard comes around the corner once in a while.

You would think that I drank forty-three beers by the look of my feet. They look like Fred Flinstone's feet. Perhaps I should have crawled over the fat Malaysian guy to go the bathroom during the flight. Kavi is sleeping and I am drinking. The Indian beer called 'Raj' tastes so good. The bottles are twice the size of Canadian bottles and they are the same strength.

I ponder. What lies ahead? Will a beautiful Indian woman come to me? Is some sort of enlightenment ahead? Will there be any good parties involved in this trek? Will I meet any cool and intelligent people? What will I learn? I can feel that this is going to be one hell of an experience.

Kavi and I eat a quick breakfast and get into an auto-rickshaw. The auto-rickshaws are neat, three wheeled affairs. They are dull yellow and are driven by little, black haired men who are often hairy. Some of the men have little red dots between their eyebrows or slightly above that spot. They speak little English and for the most part are nice guys. The vinyl roof on the rickshaw can be removed. The vehicle can get up to between fifty and sixty kilometers per hour. On busy streets it seems like ninety. They are small, efficient and have good horns. Horns are required as there are many blind corners. Horns are not just for honking at a lady who has a nice figure. We drive past a twenty-foot billboard image of John Travolta pointing a gun, advertising a movie called *Face Off*, which is one twisted diabolical movie. The street is bustling with people and filled with the noise of traffic.

We pull up to an American Express money exchange. Nervously exchanging a $100.00 Canadian for 2520 Rupees I am taken aback by the stack of bills. I turn to Kavi and ask him if all this money was for real. I soon learn that a tourist in India can easily part with a large stack of Rupees.

Phanni, Kavi's bride to be, and her father arrive to pick up Kavi and I. They drive us to the airport. They send me off and watch from the entrance. They cannot enter the airport at all because they are not travel-ing. After a few tries I find the correct line up and get my boarding pass. Kavi must be worried; he keeps waiving and pointing. He finally puts his hands down and relaxes when I walk up to the correct airline desk. I waive goodbye to Kavi and then walk into a large empty room with plastic chairs and take a seat. It is a different kind of waiting room being almost the size of an airplane hanger.

The airplane is something else. It is rickety inside and the seating is quite tight. People bump into you hard as they pass by. The plane makes rackety noises during take off. I have been on combines that make less noise than this Indian Air aircraft. I wish for a safe trip and ignore the negativity by reading and writing.

The plane touches down in Cochin shortly after 3:00 p.m.. Thank goodness the flight was just over an hour. I am meeting Kavi's father, Nogandichen, and his brother-in-law Mammea. There they are waiting outside the small sole airport terminal in the parking lot. Oh-oh, I have to be careful. Nogandichen has a briefcase tucked under his arm and is looking serious. The air is hot and extremely humid. I start to sweat and do not stop for a long while. The thought of an air-conditioned bar with cool beer dances in my head.

Nogandichen and Mammea drop me off at the Cochin Y.M.C.A. that has been reserved for me for four nights. The daily cost of the room is a little over ten dollars Canadian.

The clerk takes my deposit and takes me to the room. It is bright and clean. The bathroom is cool and spotless. The clerk states, "You should not drink alcohol in your room. Just use discretion. There is a bar not far away. It is called the Metropolitan. The restaurant downstairs is quite good. They can ring you for dinner if you wish."

"I thank you for the information Sir. I will talk to you later as I need to shop for a tie in the next few days."

"You are welcome Mr. Brent."

I set up the room and find an auto-rickshaw to take me to the Metropolitan. I feel foolish because the bar is only a block an a half down an alleyway. The bar is wood paneled, dimly lit and full of Indian men dressed differently yet similar. I feel quite alone. It is easy being the only white guy in the bar. No women, no woman no cry. I like being alone and having a beer with nothing but God, the universe and life to marvel upon. It is also nice to be able to make some journal entries.

Walking away from the Y.M.C.A. down the uneven sidewalk the thought of a tie for the wedding is persistent. As I walk towards downtown I stop and look at a large field where five young boys are playing cricket. One of the smaller boys takes the bat. He hits the ball and runs.

I meet a hustler who I will simply call The Hustler. He wants to help me find the right tie and the best rum. He is a real piece of work. I am not about to tell you about the smells, the colors, the traffic, the abundance of people traveling in so many different directions. *I will get descriptive with you Keenan when I have to. Besides, this is a crazy place with much going on.* We find the tie and then go for some beer.

The Hustler turns out to be much more than your typical dumb ass. He is so bloody stupid he takes me to a heavily guarded naval base after claiming that a military surplus store sells the best rum in the city. I go along thinking that this guy knows what he is doing and that they do sell rum in the military part of town. I did buy him a few drinks in the bar beforehand but he seemed okay. I take a photo of us in the auto-rickshaw using the extended arm method. Yes, he does end up looking half drunk. The auto-rickshaw driver takes us up to the gate of the naval base and stops, after being motioned to do so by the four guards armed with machine guns and dressed in white uniforms. I get out. I can tell we are in deep shit because of the expressions on their faces. I try to appear lost. Thank goodness I am not drunk.

"What are you doing here? You are trespassing on a military naval base!" He is angry. I think we should have stopped thirty yards back and walked up. Two of the guards take me to a large white tent just inside the fence. The Hustler cowers in the back of the auto-rickshaw. I look inside the base and do not see anything that could remotely be considered a surplus store open to the public.

The man in charge, whose rank I cannot determine, questions me.

"We came to buy rum for a wedding. I think we are in the wrong place. My guide told me that we could buy the best rum in Cochin at the base, at a military surplus store."

I talk myself out of getting arrested by glaringly pointing at The Hustler, who is now standing on the sidewalk as the auto-rickshaw driver leaves, and state apologetically, "He is my guide. I think he is drunk. He is bad guide. I am from Canada and am too trusting." This takes a few tries because I have yet to perfect my Indian accent. Need more Apu. You need to flow and somewhat musical when you enunciate your Indian English. I must remember '*WHAT THE HELL ARE YOUR DOING, GO TO THE TEMPLE AND SAY YOUR PRAYERS*'. REMEMBER HOW TO SHAKE YOUR HEAD CORRECTLY WHEN YOU ARE BEING QUESTIONED BY A GROUP OF MEN CARRYING BIG GUNS! Shaking your head "no" the way we do it in the West can mean "yes" here. Especially if you extend your neck a little and do a head wiggle. "No" can soon become "yes". I am dismissed and walk away briskly.

A block away I can see a rickshaw parked. The fat gutted Hustler tries to follow me. I move quicker and he tires. Less than a ten-minute ride later I finally find myself in front of a liquor store. *Keenan, if you are in a strange place and in need of something, ask a cabby!* After buying a case of XXX rum we drive to Mammea's knowing I should not take a case of rum into the Y.M.C.A.; not the entire case anyway.

The sky is moderately overcast with the sun peeking out through the soft white loose clouds. There are large boatyards at the far end of the canal with towering cranes for loading and unloading barges. Nogandichen and I are at the boat dock and are a little early for a boat tour of the harbor and island. On the opposite side of the boat dock is a construction site that is so intriguing that we both walk up to the fence bordering the site without saying a word to each other. The site is quite large and on ground level. It looks like a large building will be going up. They do not build underground parking here. There is no need.

Two men are making lengths of re-bar into circles by hand. They are wearing flip flop sandals. The fellow pulling on the re-bar curving machine has a bandaged head. I could have described the scene for hours; I take a picture. Construction here is clearly labor intensive and slow going.

We are out in the bay sitting on top of the boat in plastic lawn chairs. The view of Cochin is more impressive from afar. There is a mixed group here with some pale skinned British with their cup of tea accents. The clouds are slowly drifting away, allowing the heat to intensify. Two men are fishing on a rough looking boat with a square sail using long poles to move them along. We pass a naval ship. It is painted white with red lettering. There is a large machine gun turret at the bow. I look for but do not find any other guns. We cross the bay at a slow pace.

The Chinese fishing nets are eye-catching. A large blue net about seventy by seventy-five feet is suspended in the air by four poles. Three long poles are wired together to make one long pole, which acts as a cantilever. The end of the cantilever pole is attached to the ends of the four poles that are attached to the net. The structure is more than thirty feet high and is grounded to the shore with the net being suspended over the sea. The system is balanced with stones as counterweights. A large number of Chinese fishing nets line the shore. The nets sit idle except for one. There are two men checking out the ropes and pulleys on it.

"Nogandichen, do you think they will lower the net and catch some fish?" I ask.

"Those are Chinese fishing nets. They are mainly a tourist attraction. They do work but I do not know how well. They say a Chinese explorer introduced the knowledge of the nets centuries ago."

We dock for the land tour. We should be able to walk up close to the nets as long as our guide does not pull us into a church too quickly. I look down the shore and it looks like the two fisherman are getting ready to lower the net. We are taken to an old Christian Church that John the Baptist apparently blessed. At least it is cool inside.

We walk into an air-conditioned restaurant, which is our rest stop before the boat trip back. A man named Peter from England joins us for a pint. I buy a round despite Nogandichen's request to split a beer. I refuse and say, "A full beer will not last you long. We were in the heat for nearly three hours." He nods. I am correct as Nogandichen finishes his first. I order another round, which makes him grin. We stay for forty minutes, converse and enjoy our second round of beer. The beer is refreshing in taste and the mug looks attractive while it sits idle for two moments and sweats.

Someone rings me up three bloody times. I am in deep sleep. I am not sick in my body but feel tired and mildly dizzy. It could be a touch of heat stroke from the boat deck. The restaurant likely rang me wanting to know if I had supper yet. These guys eat so late. It is too late to eat out past 10:00 p.m. unless you are at a dinner party and plan to stay up until 2:00 a.m., get fat and have nightmares. What is going on here? And where are the hot dogs? (Hee, hee). Perhaps the malaria pills are making me delusional. The health nurse, before we left Canada, said that the pills had some side effects, but I do not remember her mentioning delusions. Who needs a beer with this shit going on in my head? I think it could be sunstroke. I should go out for a walk and get some fresh air.

It is a beautiful morning that warrants a nice long relaxing walkabout. It is easy to get around by foot from the Y.M.C.A. as it is central. It is nice to have a free day to do whatever I want. Free days are the best. When you only have yourself and the Creator to answer to. I walk and walk and walk some more. Nothing bothers me, not even the constant honking of the horns or the whistle of the traffic policeman. I think I have covered half of the shopping district. There are many shops that sell fabric. Street vendors line the sidewalks.

Time to check out the Hotel Lucia bar. It is getting late in the day. The waiter arrives and places a Raj and bowl of peanuts on the table. There is a middle-aged man sitting alone across the bar, facing me. We glance at each other. He waves, joins me and introduces himself.

I ask him, "Why did you come over to my table?"

Matthew answers, "It is not because you are the only white person in the bar. It is because when I saw you, I found you interesting and quite approachable. Your demeanor speaks of a humanist and you were smiling." He is a lawyer. It is a funny thing, two lawyers meeting in a bar in India.

"Matthew," I ask, "what day is it? I want to make a note of our meeting."

"Brent, it is December 19th."

"Thank you Sir."

We talk lawyer stuff, that is only interesting to lawyer types, such as colonialism and the history of British Common Law. We get along well even when we turn to religion, spirituality and history.

"You do not need religion to be spiritual." Matthew says.

I reply, "Religion, in my opinion, for the most part has been used as a tool to control the masses. I have been talking to God since I was a little boy. When I study Islam and learn that one must follow the five tenets in order to appease God, my heart aches."

Matthew states, "Islam is an intensely dogmatic and controlling religion because it is more than just a religion. It is also a political system."

After three rounds of beers; the twenty four ounce ones, Matthew invites me to go with him to court the next day.

"Meet me outside on the corner at 11:00 a.m.. Wear your suit. I do not care how hot it is, you should wear a suit and tie. I assume that you have one as you are here for a wedding."

"Do not worry. I have a good suit and tie. My only concern is getting my white shirt dirty. I will be there. Thank you for the invitation. It is a good opportunity. I am sure English is spoken in court and not Malayalam."

"English is spoken and you will be able to follow the proceedings."

The courthouse is interesting. We walk up steps on the exterior of the building to a second level. There is a walkway surrounding the rear of the structure allowing exterior access to the courtrooms. Most of the lawyers are wearing English style long black gowns. The courtroom is small and crowded. There is a little fan rotating above the dimly lit room. Three stacks of manila files, each stack three feet high, are on the judge's bench to the right.

The judge enters the room and everyone stands. He looks at me. Matthew introduces, "Your Honor, this is Mr. Bittner. He is a Canadian lawyer and is my humanist friend. Mr. Bittner, this is Justice Vaygee."

The Justice says, "Welcome to India Mr. Bittner. Thank you for visiting my courtroom and showing interest."

"Thank-you for the opportunity to observe your proceedings Sir." I respond.

Justice Vaygee takes a file off the closest stack and calls out the matter. His English is clear and he is very well spoken. He tries to move through files efficiently but is slowed down by the lawyers. Lawyers tend to talk too much in and outside the courtroom. Most of the motions involve commercial disputes. It is cool that the proceedings are in English and one can follow the applications and argument.

I meet a number of lawyers, many who are younger, who are interested as to what I am doing here as I wait for Matthew's matter to be called. All of a sudden, Justice Vaygee starts talking in Malayalam. It turns out that the young lawyer requesting an order is not familiar with the file. He gets a talking to for not being prepared.

The judge then explains to me, "Mr. Bittner. I spoke in our native tongue because I did not want to embarrass the young man for not being prepared. It is nothing on you."

I stand and say, "That is okay Sir, many young lawyers in Edmonton find themselves in court being unprepared as they did not take time to review another lawyer's file, or because of their own procrastination."

Matthew's matter is called. He is trying to convince the Court to take a freeze off of a client's assets. An order is in place that prevents his client from using funds in a bank account. The Defendant banker is afraid that the Plaintiff, Matthew's client, may skip town before the action goes to trial.

Matthew and I have a good discussion about law over lunch. We ask the waiter to take our photo. It is Friday afternoon and Matthew will not be going back to work. He asks me, "Brent, do you want to go out to the country this weekend and meet my wife and family?"

"That is a good idea and generous invitation, however, I am leaving town in two days."

"That is too bad Brent. It is a nice country home with peaceful surroundings. My wife would certainly enjoy meeting you and cooking for us."

"Well, I have your business card. I will be coming back to India. Can I take you up on the offer on a later date?"

"Yes, of course. Just do not wait until I am an old man who cannot enjoy a beer with a friend."

I will see Matthew again.

It is mid-afternoon and I am sitting on the outside steps of the hostel looking out at the traffic with a bored look on my face. I wish that I could have gone to Matthew's home. He has a good brain and soul. A well built, good looking Indian fellow is walking by. He looks toward me and waves. He walks up and introduces himself.

"Hello Sir. My name is Sammi."

"Hi. I am Brent." I stand up and shake his hand and note his eyes.

"What brings you to Cochin?"

"I am going to my best friend Kavi's wedding. I cannot tell you the town. Only that it is near Chakkalamannil house, which is Kavi's family home. Don't ask me to spell it."

"Where are you from and what do you do?"

"I am from Canada and I am a lawyer."

"Isn't that interesting? I am studying for my Masters in Law. It is exciting to meet a Canadian lawyer."

"Well, it is exciting for me to run into a second person here in two days who has chosen the legal profession."

"What do you mean?" asks Sammi.

"I went to court today with a lawyer named Matthew."

"Good for you to go to court. How did you meet this Matthew?" he asks inquisitively.

"I met Matthew at the Hotel Lucia bar."

"So you like to drink. Let me buy you dinner tonight. I want to hear your story. I have to leave but I will return at 8:00 p.m. to meet you."

"Sounds good to me. I want to hear your story also. Looking forward to it."

Sammi greets me on the steps and we leave for the restaurant in an auto-rickshaw. It is a very nice candle lit place on the second floor of a building. A mild waft of incense passes us. We are served generic pop and Sammi pulls out a mickey of rum.

Sammi looks at menu. "Brent, do you like hot food?"

"Yes. As long as it is not so hot that tears pour out of my eyes. I do not mind if it makes me sweat some."

Sammi orders and while we wait he tells me of his experiences in law school and undergraduate studies. He is a well spoken pleasant man.

The food arrives. We are treated to two different types of rice, a chicken curry and a lamb curry along with some sides.

I say, *"LET'S HURRY BECAUSE I JUST LOVE MY CHICKEN CURRY."*

Sammi replies, "That is a good accent Mr. Brent. I enjoy my chicken curry in a hurry also."

The food is great. The best meal yet on this trek.

Sammi tells me of a time when he was in the home of an American host a few years ago. Sammi was on a one month school exchange. A married father with a couple kids fondled Sammi's sausage while he was sleeping!

"He did not look like a gay Brent. He seemed to be a happy family man who loved his wife. He was a bit of a dork though and not very masculine. He poured the drinks heavy and I passed out on the basement sofa."

"What did you do when you woke up?" I ask.

"I grabbed his wrist and squeezed the hell out of it and looked him in the face like I was going to kill him."

"I am sure he got the message."

Sammi says, "He got the message alright. You should have seen how sheepish he was around the kitchen having coffee, bacon and pancakes in the morning."

"Did you play with the situation at all; such as grabbing your package, shaking your head side to side, mouthing "no, no, no," to him, while out of sight of his family?"

"That is funny. I wish that I would have thought of that. I was not there for that long and he left me alone after the incident. Some people simply do not have a conscience."

"Sammi, that is right. Some people are simply evil and put their own selfish sick desires over the good of others." I feel like telling him about a couple of sick dick heads that I have come across but do not. Instead I tell Sammi the testicle story; after we are finished eating.

You know Keenan it's kind of funny when you think about it. You end up in a city in India that is not a big tourist destination. You have an Old Fort, St. Francis Church, a palace and a synagogue. Oh yes, don't forget the Chinese fishing nets. Yet I run into a lawyer and a law student and have a great time with both of them as I am like-minded with both. Life can be so wonderful. When I take you to India we will have to look up both Matthew and Sammi ahead of time so we can spend a few days with each of them.

I sleep in until 9:30 a.m. and count the Rupees.

> This monopoly money drives me loon
> waiting to see the cost of the room
> twenty-five Rupees for a Canadian dollar
> wishing my feet were a tad bit smaller
> You learn to be tight in a foreign land
> threaten to slap the rogue with an open hand
> calm prevails as it should
> the vendor recants and makes good.

It is a new day and I feel great. I pack my things after returning from breakfast. The timing is good. Just as I finish packing, and do a last minute check, Nogandichen and Mammea come by and pick me up. Mammea and I talk about my experiences over the past few days.

We get our train tickets and wait for the train. Nogandichen and I are going to Kavi's Uncle George's house. I buy some fruit drinks for us. Mammea and Nogandichen look like a couple of school boys with their juice boxes in their hands and their legs hanging down from the high bench. I see an overweight porter and ask him to take our picture. It is always best to get an overweight person to take your photo; someone who cannot outrun you with your camera in hand.

We have tickets for seats in second-class air conditioning. Nogandichen knows his tickets. He was a conductor by profession before he gave it up to move to Canada. The seats are well cushioned but it is a little too cool for shorts. I end up spending a lot of time between the cars taking in the scenery and enjoying the heated breeze pass through.

Uncle George

The train comes to a stop in a small town called Edayaranmula. There is no station beside the track, just a small platform. We get off the train and lug our bags across a ditch and onto a dusty road. Nogandichen waves the first cab driver away because he is too expensive. He says, "Brent, you have to bargain with everyone here and bargain well."

We arrive at Uncle George's. He has a large house. It is concrete and painted white. There are six steps leading up to a spacious open veranda that runs the width of the front of the house. I am shown to my room and unpack and store what is left of the rum. Seven full bottles remain. I will be sharing a room with Kavi. He will be coming by train tomorrow. A curtain can be drawn to separate our beds. The room is bright, spacious and very clean. Window openings face the side and back yards. It is a nice room with a large alcove to store my things.

George Lukose is a large stoic man. He wears thick glasses with large frames. His hair is gray and receded but he does not yet have a shiny crown. He wears a white lungi and no shirt. Uncle George appears to be quite intelligent and at peace with himself. He retired from the Kerala Oil and Natural Gas Commission where he was the Superintending Palynologist. He will become my Uncle George.

Most of my time is spent on the veranda reading and writing in the shade, where you can see two streets. A gate to the left, at the end of a driveway prevents people from entering the yard. Uncle George's black four-door sedan is parked at the front of the driveway, which is to the right of the veranda. A bottle of rum and a large bottle of Pepsi are beside my feet. Uncle George is sitting in a chair beside me. A half glass of rum and Pepsi sits on the one-foot concrete ledge of the veranda that serves as my table. The sun is setting.

Uncle George puts an empty glass beside mine. I mix him a drink the real man way, one-third rum, two-thirds Pepsi, with no ice because it is hard to come by. He is not the type of man to smile. He is so damn serious, but he smiles and pats me on the shoulder. We both take a long drink and start talking.

Uncle George says, "The electrical grid needs to power itself up because the people have used so much electricity before and during the supper hour. That is why we always eat after the light comes back on." He places a lit candle on the ledge between our glasses.

I ask, "Uncle George, I hope that I can call you Uncle George." He nods. "Are you enjoying your retirement?"

"I do enjoy being retired but I must keep busy. Let me show you my hobby." He opens a door to a small room that is adjacent to the veranda. There are dozens of bottles of homeopathic medicines. Uncle George explains some of their qualities.

We sit down and Uncle George asks, "Do you like being a lawyer in Canada?"

"Yes. I enjoy helping people and like running litigation trials with contractual issues. The drawback is that lawyers from big firms fight blindly, trying to convince you that you that your client does not have a strong case. It is especially funny when lawyers with skinny necks, who cannot fill a suit properly, try to browbeat me."

"That is because the profession draws many people who crave power and have big egos; but not you. You have spirit. I can tell."

"Thank you."

Nogandichen comes out and places a glass on the ledge.

We eat late, talk and then go to bed. The bed is comfortable and the sleep is good.

Uncle George, Kavi's mom Tarah, Nogandichen and I leave for the train station to meet Kavi and Phanni. They are late. No, the train is late. Indian time is like Mexican time. In the West, we crucify ourselves with time. The more technologically advanced we get with email, internet, couriers and the like the more demanding people become; they expect you to return their message within an hour. Phanni goes to stay with an Aunt while Kavi and I catch up on events while sitting on the roof of Uncle George's house. The heat is extremely intense up here and we are forced to seek shade after twenty minutes.

I wake up after a nap. I find out that almost everyone has gone out to shop for a wedding ring. Uncle George's daughter, Binna and Mrs. Lukose remain. It is a good time for some *Moby Dick* and some rum. Reading, pouring another drink of rum … I think they know that I am starting to tie one on. I return to the fridge for another bottle of Pepsi.

A slight heat rash and a sore lower back do not take away my general feeling of happiness. Business is virtually out of my mind. I feel so happy to be alone with the quiet, soft nature. I hear birds sing and feel a soft wind. It is not as hot and humid as it was earlier. I should not have spent so much time on the roof this morning with Kavi. I need to cool off.

Bluish-grey clouds roll in. I walk out to the road to greet the hard rain, dancing while large droplets beat on my face and bare chest. Thank you Creator for the rain. Mrs. Lukose sees me through the open top half of the two-part door. I look up and talk to God and am thankful for the cool refreshing rain. I turn to Mrs. Lukose and wave. She looks at me like I am crazy. I look up and feel the rain splash against my face. I can have a cool shower anytime but this is priceless. It is much cooler and I do not need to be concerned with the amount of water I use. Life is fabulous.

My behavior must have been reported to Nogandichen. As soon as he returns, I see him head straight to my room. He calls out, "Brent, come to your room please!"

I go to my room and ask, "What is wrong Nogandichen."

"How much rum did you drink this afternoon?" He sees a bottle that is two thirds gone. "Oh my God! You drank that much rum by yourself! You cannot do that!"

"Hey. First of all it is weak rum. I am used to rum that is twice as strong. Secondly, I did not interfere with anyone's person or their property. Therefore, I have done no wrong. Thirdly, I am not drunk but feeling good. Drunkenness requires slurred speech and loss of motor coordination. Lastly, it is my rum. If I have offended our gracious hosts in anyway please let it be known." I look behind me and see Uncle George grinning from ear to ear. I can tell he enjoys the fact that I stand up to Nogandichen's bossy behavior.

At dinner I learn the culture of naming children. All of the first-born receive their father's mother's name or the father's father's name. The second born receives the mother's father's or mother's mother's name. The third born receives their first uncle's name or the paternal aunt's name.

Uncle George and Kavi continue to explain and you can see that Nogandichen wants to hold court. He interrupts and holds up one of those mini bananas in his left hand. "Brent. What is this?" He is sitting next to me on the left.

"It is a pappadum."

The little bugger then moves his right hand fast trying to cuff me in the back of the head. I move my head forward and down while he overextends and almost comes out of his chair onto the table.

"What the hell was that for?" I ask with a bit of aggression. There are looks of surprise across the table.

"Haven't you learned anything that I have taught you. A pappadum is not even a fruit! It is a fried chip made from lentil flour." Nogandichen explains angrily.

"At least I am close, both are Indian foods." This breaks the tension at the table as Kavi and Uncle George laugh. The ladies at the table also find the situation humorous. The thought of a little seventy year old man, weighing one hundred and forty pounds, who looks almost identical to Ghandi if it was not for his rice tummy; taking a swat at a man much taller and sixty pounds heavier is too funny.

I am not upset. Nevertheless the incident makes my decision much easier. I will not travel with Nogandichen after the wedding. I will go it alone.

Abraham walks by on the road adjacent to Uncle George's house. Abraham is a brother to Uncle George and Tarah. It is mid-morning and Abraham casts a long shadow. He has an enticing smile. He approaches and I wave to him.

I later learn that Abraham wanted to sit down and have a drink with me. Contrary to the fact that someone, who will remain unnamed, advised me that he was against drinking. It is too bad that Abraham does not speak English. I can tell that he wants a drink as he leans against the veranda and smiles like a boy anticipating an ice cream cone in July. I want to talk to him about his daughter, his culture, and his family. I want to know what makes him tick. Uncle George could interpret.

As Abraham leaves Kavi comes out to the veranda and asks me if I want to go for a walk and see part of the town.

"What is the symbol on that front of that large house Kavi?".

"That is a Hindu symbol." Kavi explains as we walk past homes and approach the edge of town. "Therefore people will know it is a Hindu's house."

We continue walking past homes and then approach the edge of town.

"Wow, look at him. He is so beautiful Kavi. I must take a couple pictures of him." My first elephant in India. Big white tusks and all. I move a little closer and stop.

"You are a beautiful creature of God. Will you open your ears for me?" I ask quietly. The great beast does and I snap the camera. My camera does not have a zoom feature so I move closer. He is chained to a post and a large bracelet surrounds his back right ankle. I do not want to upset him. I stop moving toward him when he starts to raise his front left leg. The camera clicks.

"Kavi. Boo haaaa. Thanks for the walk. This alone makes it worthwhile."

"They should be good pictures."

"Thank you man. Thank you for bringing me here Kavi. I know it is going to be a great experience. I do not know about traveling North with your father though. He gets on my nerves."

"You are welcome but I did not bring you. You paid for your own flight and got on the plane on your own free will."

"Yes, I know. I am talking about the invitation and being put up by your family for two weeks. Plus the education on getting along in India is invaluable."

"I will not mind if you travel without my father."

We come to another elephant. Three mahouts are lounging around the front porch of what looks like a former store while a fourth mahout feeds the elephant through a window opening. Two cute little girls and a boy about six years old run up to us. I take their picture with Kavi.

Kavi says, "You see that the mahouts are wearing orange lungi's. They are Hindu monk mahouts charged with caring for this elephant. The elephant belongs to a temple and she earns the temple income."

Uncle George's house is in view when we come across a small, rickety vendor's shack. It is a cigarette and tea stand. A couple of seedy looking characters give me the eye. The guy behind the counter does not look too honest either. I will have to watch out for them.

It is a hot night and supper is good. Uncle George and I find ourselves on the couch wearing our lungis. Kavi takes our picture. Uncle George is somewhat bemused. I do not think he likes his picture taken. Then all of a sudden, Lalu walks into the living room. She must get her smile from her father Abraham. Her smile and grace is so feminine. She is utterly gorgeous. As thin as she is, like I mean arms almost as thin as a Ukrainian sausage ring—the three-inch kind, she radiates beauty. She stops, turns like she is doing a pirouette, faces me for a moment and gives me a huge smile. She then turns and walks out.

Uncle George takes a book from a shelf and hands it to me. He is the author. I ask him questions about his book. It is deep geology that covers rock formations in Kerala over the ages. He gives me the low down and then turns to his coin collection. There is a sheet of glass covering the coffee table in front of us. Coins from all over the world are scattered about. *Keenan, you would like his collection. It may not be as large as yours but it is diverse.* There are no Canadian coins. I excuse myself to retrieve my shaving kit. I pick out and hand Uncle George one of each of our Canadian coins; except our silver dollar and fifty cent piece.

I mix a couple of rum and cokes and we walk out front to the veranda. *Moby Dick* is laying on the ledge.

"How is the book?" asks Uncle George.

I reply, "It is very good. The author refers to the story of Jonah in the Old Testament. I still do not understand why Jonah was so afraid of God."

"Jonah is afraid of what may happen to him if he fails God's wishes."

"I understand."

"I see that you have written many notes for your book since you arrived. Make sure you wait at least two years or more before you write the book. You need to let your experiences sink in. Many events in life are best explained years later."

We have been sitting on the veranda for a good hour and a half. Mrs. Lukose comes out and gives Uncle George heck in Malayalam. Turns out he is on medication and Mrs. Lukose thinks that he should not be drinking at all. A few years later, when Kavi advises me of his death, he tells me that Uncle George had cancer at the time but did not tell anyone outside of his immediate family.

Not only am I thankful for his incredible insight and wisdom but for the comfortable bed, ice box, cold Pepsi, nice shower, great food and then some.

Keenan it is the morning of December 23. Two days before Christmas. Christmas is not in the air here without decorations or anything resembling a Christmas in the West. I do not miss the commercial stuff. We are sure to celebrate Christmas in one way or another.

I am going to tone down the evening drinks for a while. I have to get into shape for a week of abstinence because we are moving on to Kavi's paternal uncle's place on the day after Christmas (they don't have Boxing Day here—which is good). His name is Kutikkukachen. I will refer to him as 'Kuti'. I have been warned many times that in no event can I take a drink while at Kuti's nor should I let him know that I have rum. In fact, I have to leave the rum with Uncle George.

On occasion, abstaining from alcohol Keenan, is often a good thing. Not only can you think clearly all day; sometimes you can think clearly the next. Trouble is, if you are not in a good mood you can be toast. For some, only booze, cigarettes, pot, prescription or other drugs help them with their moods. The key is to wake up happy and not let anything or anyone piss you off. Before you judge, keep in mind that there is a big difference between liking something and needing something. You do not 'need' something if you can walk away from it for days or weeks. What I am saying kid, is that I really like to drink and do not give a crap about what anyone else has to say about it (except my mother of course). I am also saying that I hope that you do not drink as much as I do. You do not need booze to make you happy but it sure as hell helps to make people happier and more relaxed if they are having a party.

We have lunch at Abrahams. It is a well-kept and newly painted house. It was raised up four feet from the foundation a few decades ago. There is a rice silo type room right above the living room. Lalu proudly points to it and explains with single words and motions that it is a grain chest. She smiles as she steps up and opens the door displaying an abundance of rice.

Abraham sits in an easy chair, which he made himself. It has very long armrests that are wide enough to sufficiently allow one to sit all the way back and rest your legs on the armrest. He is proud of the chair. You can see it in his eyes. He should be proud. It is quite a groovy chair.

It is late morning on Christmas Eve and I feel that a big walk would be nice just now. Perhaps Kavi is up to it. He is and off we go. We are walking along a grown in path. Kavi is quiet and does not say where we are going. We come up to Tarah's house that she inherited. It is grown in with palm trees, mango trees and thick bush. You can only see a third of the little house. There is no road nearby so it would be difficult to live here.

We are walking back and on the left hand side of the gravel road is a large shop with four guys standing around, just outside the entrance. Two men are inside working on a small machine. We stop. I turn toward them slowly on my heels while I grab my camera out of my pocket and take their picture in a motion imitating a cowboy preparing for a gunfight. One guy exhales cigarette smoke and another man in his twenties, furthest to the left wears a green lungi that is hiked up to his knee, holds his left hand in a pistol position. He looks serious like Clint Eastwood before he draws his pistol in a Western shot em up. The guy in the cute purple flower lungi, furthest to the right, has his hands on his hips and is laughing. Their eyes focus on me, and I snap the picture.

The smoker and cowboy do not look pleased with the snapshot. One guy leaning against the wall is indifferent. The laughing guy is either laughing at the whitey or the fact that I have the balls to stop and take their picture like they are animals on display. Not to take any chances here, I do not want Kavi to get a black eye before his wedding. I take a little bow, blow the non-existing smoke of my camera, call out "thank you" and wave goodbye.

We pass a beautiful green field full of long grass with small groups of coconut palms. It is the most serene sight I have witnessed since being in India. There are three-foot bushes that circle the groups of palms. The only sign of man are the power lines above. Without the power lines one would say that it is a field of Eden.

Kavi and I have short naps after our walk. It is good to have siesta during the hottest part of the day when you are in the tropics and do not have an ocean to cool off in. It is easy to nap during the afternoon. All you need is a book with small print.

Mrs. Lukose cooks excellent food. Nogandichen says that they use to much oil and fat. Hah to that! It tastes great, we eat well and the food is much healthier than the food most Westerners sustain themselves with. It is a good thing that I eat well here because when we end up at the paternal Uncle Kuti's, the whitey will lose weight and end up with Fire.

It is quite dark now with the power off. All is quiet. A candle facilitates my reading and writing. The nightly power outage is expected and therefore easy to tolerate. It is actually enjoyable to have darkness and read by candlelight.

I hear singing in the distance. There is a group of young people singing what I think are Christmas Carols. They start dancing as they approach the house. I look at them inquisitively. There are eight people in the group wearing bright red and orange costumes, while some wear cloth masks. One young man is dressed like Santa. Uncle George and the others come outside as the revelers walk through the open gate.

Santa prances, and dances in circles in front of me so I join him or her. It is a funny two minutes. I donate a twenty-rupee note after getting the nod from Uncle George. One of the young men writes out a receipt for me, and says that they are raising money for a youth group. We do get a little Christmas after all.

Merry Christmas. It is early, around 8:30 a.m.. Hindu music is blaring across the far road. "Boom. Boom. Aheeehaa. Aheeehaa. Mumbina Mumbina. Aheeehaa. Boom. Boom."

Kavi and I awake. "Kavi, what the hell is going on?"

"It is the Hindu music from the loud speaker across the road."

"I can understand playing it in the late morning, but at 8:30 a.m. on Christmas day? Let's go give them hell."

Kavi is as fired up as I am. "Let's go."

We jump up, dress quickly, and march past the kitchen.

"Where are you two going? Don't make trouble with the Hindu's," Tarah warns. The two families are around the breakfast table.

"We should not have to put up with that loud noise." Kavi complains.

Uncle George settles us by stating, "You will be leaving here. I am staying here. If you cause trouble it is a reflection upon my house." Uncle George advises that some of the locals went to court to try to stop them from blasting the harsh sounds, but failed. They have freedom of expression in India too.

I am sitting on the veranda thinking about Christmas dinners as a child. I also think about making a few Christmas dinners myself while on my own. *Cooking Christmas dinner Keenan, from a real man's point of view, requires much attention to the gravy and stuffing for they are the most important sides. If you do not want your girlfriend or wife to screw up the gravy or the stuffing, cook the damn turkey yourself. Do not shut out your loved one however, you may need help with the gravy. Making good gravy takes patience* and timing. If you need some advice from your mother, do not telephone her in front of your lady. Do it secretly in the bathroom or she may be insulted.

Cooking is not at all that difficult. You just follow the directions but do not be anal about it. Own a good cookbook, the older the better—simplicity. The key factor with cooking is spicing and timing; timing and spicing. It is always good to throw in the extra dash of spice, especially pepper, for good measure. Who wants bland food unless you are cooking for residents of a nursing home.

When chopping the onion and celery for the stuffing, take your time. Finely chop with a good knife. No matter what your wife says you have to spend at least thirty dollars on a good chopping knife. Have a brown cow (half glass of milk, two ounces of Kahlua and two ounces Irish cream) for lunch with a cigar. This will put you in a nice mellow mood for chopping. This method only works once you have reached your thirties and have good experience.

After you clean the bird and because it is Christmas day, ensure that you get the obligatory photo of you and the turkey. Place your right hand inside the turkey and make the bird dance by jerking your arm up and down. Since your wife is laughing hysterically at your unusual antics for the sober hour of twelve-noon (little does she know) she wants to get involved in the fun. While you always knew that she would <u>mow your grass</u> and take over the end game of Christmas dinner preparation, you welcome her into the kitchen with a big hug and kiss.

You know that it is a big pain in the ass to peel a pot full of potatoes and a coconut hard turnip. Your lady then decides to prepare the broccoli and cheese dishes in advance, as well as the peas. After you tell her that it is a great idea, you stay within earshot while reading your new book. She will have no problem peeling your potatoes and turnip if you stay around in case she needs help.

A few hours later you take the lid off the roaster and baste the turkey and continue to do so every thirty minutes until it is done. The skin must be brown yet not crisp. At this time you offer to mash the potatoes and fluff them up with a little bit of milk.

This method of cooperative cooking with your spouse or girlfriend can also work well with barbeques. You attend the barbeque outside on the terrace in solitude, with a cocktail and cigar, while your lady makes a salad and vegetables in the kitchen. Of course you make her a perfect martini before heading *out to the patio. To keep the program going for years, all you have to do is write her a poem, entitled, 'You Make the Salad and I Will Cook the Meat'.*

We are leaving for Kuti's later this afternoon. My experience in India has been pretty damn good so far. Some aspects of India are troubling but it's not difficult at all to lose a negative thought after a few moments. India allows me to forget about the 'go, go go' of the West. You can slow down and appreciate life here. It does not seem that it is just India that has brought a deeper sense of awareness. I have found and caught the wave of life's energy and am flowing with her. Being positive and jolly comes easy if you block out the negative and embrace the positive energy that permeates everything in life. I am looking forward to the wedding.

The Achen Kovil River

Kavi, his parents and I leave for Kuti's around 6 p.m.. Kuti drives his own taxi and has a beer gut that is big, round and firm. Don't get me wrong, he is not at all fat. He is not like one of those heavy guys who has a gut pouring over his rodeo belt buckle and a plumber's butt in the rear. He is of medium build and does not have any fat hanging down or muscle sag. His shirtless body reveals a round tanned basketball tummy. His stomach is the best specimen of an ultimate firm beer boiler I have ever seen.

While eating late, right away I am blessed with big time runs. Kuti laughs madly at me. He takes great pleasure in seeing me suffer. He calls my predicament <u>Big Fire</u>. I would kick his butt if my tract was not aflame. I see what is going on with the food here. It is a little crappy so they spice it up so much that it has a good, hot, taste. Trouble is, the fish look like little monster fish; miniature piranhas with huge teeth. Instead of eating Christmas dinner I am eating deep fried piranha minnows, which is like eating something such as chicken feet. What is the point? There is no food there. A man needs food. Men eat better after a night in the drunk-tank. At least there is plenty of rice on the table and that is good.

The next morning I awake hot. Like most mornings I want to cool off and get clean so I go down to the river for a swim before breakfast. It is called the *Achen Kovil River*. It is a stress free river to swim in. It is reasonably clean with a medium current just strong enough that I can swim against it at an easy pace and remain in the same spot.

There is not much to do at Kuti's except swim in the river and read under the shade of a tree. Even though the house is partially shaded by tall fruit producing palms, it is hot during the day, particularly if there is no breeze. There is extra high humidity because we are next to the river. The house is small and I feel crowded. Kuti's wife and daughter do not speak

English at all, leaving uncomfortable moments during the day when Kavi and his parents are away.

It is early afternoon and no one is around. Kavi and his parents are gone for most of the day to prepare for the wedding. It is very hot and super humid. It feels like the temperature is close to forty degrees Celsius. I have been swimming for more than an hour. I swim to shore for a break and see Kuti bringing his cow down to the river for a wash. I run and get my camera and take a shot of him washing the cows back. The cow appears to enjoy the coolness of the river.

It is shortly before dusk and I am inside the house reading while Kavi and his parents are sitting around the kitchen table discussing the wedding reception. Kuti calls out from the riverbank, "Mr. Brent. Come here. I want to show you how to fish."

"Okay, on the way boss." I call yell back. I have seen the metal wires imbedded in the river's bottom and bank and am therefore curious to see how he fishes. It sure the hell isn't with a rod and reel. You could not get last nights fish on a hook unless you were to slide it on as if it were bait.

I find Kuti down at the riverbank with an extension cord and flashlight in one hand and a small catch net in the other. "First, I make sure that the ground wire is in place."

He wiggles it a bit and it looks firm. "Okay, good. Notice that I place the net right beside me on the bank. When the sun goes down I will put the power on. I touch these two wires together and give the water a jolt."

I think that if he jolts the water too hard that the baby may drop out of his stomach. I go with a better joke and ask Kuti in a serious voice and straight face, "Kuti, is that why the power goes out in India for an hour after dark each night?"

He glares and states, "Are you trying to be funny Mr. Brent?"

"Yes, I am. How do you know when to jolt the water?"

"I shine the flashlight. The fish get startled and hesitate, then I zap them."

Keenan, I am so damn tempted to ask him if he ever catches a big one that he could actually filet and not fry to crisp. I do not because I am a guest at his house and will do my best not to complain about the food. On the other hand, I could ask Nogandichen if we could to buy some chickens and make a big batch of chicken curry.

Sure as shit, a small school comes by and Kuti shines the light, then quickly puts the light under his chin and touches the wires together, and then, Zap! He drops the wires, grabs the catch net and scoops up about nine six inch fish. Thank you river for not delivering the piranha types.

The dinner is okay. We are eating fish, rice and mini-bananas. The spice level is super high. We are eating late. Oh Oh. "Excuse me please." I move quickly to the outhouse and take my time. No toilet paper here. The water jug method works good and cools, but not for long.

I return to the table and take my seat. Kuti does not waste any time and asks me with sarcasm, "Mr. Brent. Do you have Big Fire again?"

"Yes, but not near as bad as last night." I reply. The fish is a bit better but hotter. I am getting to like the hot. My digestive system just needs some catching up. Nogandichen and Kuti start to talk between themselves in Malayalam. You can tell that they are making fun of me. I hear the word 'saipe' often, which Kavi taught me earlier. It is a derogatory term for white people. White people are mocked by many Indians because we use toilet paper. The use of toilet paper here is considered dirty resulting in being labeled an unclean person.

I look at Kavi to see if he is listening as he knows Malayalam fairly well. The conversation cannot be that bad as Kavi does not say anything. Perhaps he is seeing how far Kuti and Nogandichen will go on the 'saipe' stuff. *More often or not someone who bullies or cuts another person down lacks self esteem and love. Do not get defensive with them. If they engage you ask them why they do not love thyself and have to act so foolish.*

It is a bright beautiful new day this morning with no sign of the Big Fire. Yogurt or goat milk is the key to counteracting the curry. We drive to the train station in Kuti's cab. Jobe and Pengal arrive almost on time. The wedding rehearsal is later this afternoon and they are required company. Pengal is a bridesmaid and Jobe a groomsman.

The wedding rehearsal is going well. Most of the decisions have been made. We walk down the aisle the regular Western way and stand where told. My job is to escort Phanni's sister down the aisle, look good, breathe slow and not faint. Then the Christian Kerala customs kick in. It is not your routine wedding rehearsal. It is an Indian traditional Christian wedding blended in with a few Western customs. Standing to the far left of Kavi I watch him as he practices doing the thread thing. He has to take three threads from Phanni's sari, twine them together, thread it through a small hole in a pendant, tie a knot that a seasoned cub scout would have trouble with and then tie the pendant around her neck in an important and special way.

I bet you that this is where the expression 'tie the knot' originates. Is this something to make the groom more fearful of getting married? Getting married is fearful enough. If grooms in the West had to pass the thread tying test we would have a lot less divorces. Kavi does well with the knot.

The Wedding

The church is now standing room only. Kavi patiently stands to my right at the front of the church, waiting for Phanni to walk up the aisle. There are about a hundred people seated and many more standing around outside the church looking through the windows. There is not much airflow in here. I cannot faint. Why the hell am I worried, I am not the one who has to tie the knot.

Oh my goodness, you should see Lalu! She may be the most beautiful young woman I have ever seen. Her long shiny black hair is pulled back away from her lovely face revealing her high cheekbones. Her wide smile exposes gleaming pure white teeth. She wears very little makeup and she doesn't need any. She has a perfect thin nose and bright brown eyes. Her lips are just right, not thin or puffy. Our eyes meet and she smiles. Lalu is wearing a purple sari that is just gorgeous. I am not into women's fashion but this outfit fits and flows on her like a princess.

The processional music begins and Phanni begins to walk down the aisle with her father. She looks very happy. Kavi is proudly standing tall. The service ends quickly with moments of timelessness even while watching Kavi loop and tie the knot.

The reception hall is huge enough to park a 747. There are more than five hundred people seated. I am seating beside the Minister on his left. Our table for two is angled on the large stage. Kavi and Phanni are sitting across from us at a similar angle. There is a middle table with the couple's parents. The stage is about eight feet above the floor, facing the crowd of people anxiously waiting to be served lunch.

I look down at my setting. Just a I thought, there is no fork or cutlery. I am not practiced up enough to eat in front of a big group yet. I am surely to choke. The Minister stands, walks to the podium and says grace. All of us on the stage are now being served. I look about and conclude that I am the only white person here.

I am half way through the meal when a piece of hot, boney chicken curry lodges in my throat. I am choking so badly that tears are streaming down my crimson red face. Need water. Don't you dare choke to death, not here and not now. I turn toward the back of the stage and using my right hand and smack myself right in the middle of my chest. Thump! I can breathe now. It seems only the Minister noticed as he hands me his water.

The speeches are about to start. Many of the people are leaving. How rude, they just came for a free meal. I have written out a quick speech. It is not nearly as long as Nogandichen's. I get up and walk over to the podium. Thank goodness for water and the time to recover from the choking scene. I get to the podium and begin to read:

"I first met Kavi one fall when I was 28 years old. We became friends. We soon became best friends. From playing billiards together, intellectual conversations, exchanging dreams and sharing a flat together, I can say that I am in a position to tell you this about Kavi. He is the best friend one could ever have. He is a gentleman. He has a warm and caring heart. I know that Kavi will make an excellent husband for you Phanni. Although he may not enjoy washing dishes, he can cook two or three meals pretty well. If you have trouble getting his help with washing dishes, ask him to buy you a dishwasher. Kavi really enjoys billiards and drinking beer. So Phanni, you ought to learn to play. I am sure that he will be a great teacher and you Phanni a mediocre student. Kavi has been an excellent best friend. Now you are Kavi's best friend Phanni. I wish you both the best. Thank you."

Not much of a response from the crowd. That is okay. Kavi and Phanni appreciate the thoughts. I will be allowed the opportunity to rock a much more receptive crowd back home next summer, as their Master of Ceremonies, at their Edmonton wedding reception. It will be easy to make the crowd piss themselves laughing. All I have to do is start with the choking story and take it from there. An English speaking crowd and plenty of libation will not hurt either. I can imagine it right now by starting out with,

WELCOME TO KAVI'S AND PHANNI'S EDMONTON WEDDING RECEPTION, HOW THE HELL ARE YOU ALL DOING?

I knew that there would not be alcohol at this reception. It does not fit in with the culture. Nor could one afford to provide alcohol for everyone unless you convinced Jesus to attend, renew his vows with Mary Magdalene, and turn tap water into three thousand bottles of wine.

The wedding party and remaining guests congregate in various groups outside the hall and talk like hell. I decide to sneak away and find a bar. I ask a taxi driver arranged by Kuti to take me to the nearest bar. He drops me off and I walk into the Raj. After sitting down and ordering a beer I take note. I like to people watch but here it is difficult. A few of the fellows sitting on stools and standing at the bar, enjoying their afternoon beer, apparently have never seen a white man. They are staring at me, but not in a threatening manner. One fellow has seen a white man before. He is a tough looking guy with a muscular build and looks about thirty. He is holding court with his buddies. After an awkward seven or eight minutes he comes over and takes a seat across from me.

"Excuse me. Do you mind if I join you?"

"No, not at all."

"My name is Biyar. I know you are wondering why my friends are staring at you. They can count the white people that they have seen on both hands."

"My name is Brent. Can I buy you a beer?"

"No, but I can buy you a beer and have some nuts brought over."

Biyar asks me about the wedding ceremony. He then tells me about his town and what he does. He turns out to be a nice guy. I thought there was slight chance that he wanted to try to kick my ass in front of his buddies in order to impress them. Biyar leaves my table after a beer and rejoins his friends. They no longer stare.

I think that Kavi and his family might be worried about where I am. No worry as Kavi will figure it out. Every wedding should have a party. I do not care who you are or where you are from. It reminds me of my one sister's wedding years ago. She married a Pentecostal minister right out of high school. Not only was it a dry wedding reception but her husband could not even dance at his own wedding. No drinking and no dancing if you are Pentecostal. Prove to me that God forbids alcohol consumption or dancing. It cannot be done.

Biyar and his gang have left. I decide to have another beer and write some more notes. Perhaps I should try to find another venue that is on the way back home to Chikalamanil House, something with a patio or deck with a view.

I get up and pay the tab with tip. As soon as I walk out the door I see a Hindu taxi driver. How do I know that he is Hindu? He has a small Ganesh (one of the main Hindu deities that resembles and elephant with human features) on his dashboard. I explain my end destination and that I would like to stop at a bar on the way. We drive off after exchanging names.

"Gavi, do you like beer?" I ask. He gives the yes head nod. It is a good nod. Bet his head goes up seven inches and he wiggles his eyes. That is another reason that I like Hindu's more than Pentecostal's. Hindu teachings do not result in hypocritical rules and dogma.

"Let us stop on the way. Do you know of a restaurant or bar on the way that has a patio with a view Sir?" I ask.

"Mr. Brent, I know place. Not far down road."

"Gavi. Would you like a cigarette?"

"Yes." I light it for him, being careful not to wet lip it, and pass it to him. I light one for myself and marvel at the idea of going for beers with a Hindu auto-rickshaw driver who likes beer and cigarettes.

We arrive at a small hotel with a second floor patio and restaurant. I love open air patio restaurants, especially if you can see vehicle and pedestrian traffic go by. It is a clean upscale looking place with white concrete and red trim. It is well decorated.

I order a round of beers. Gavi teaches me about Hinduism. He says, "Hinduism is all embracing. It is about love of life. There is the supreme being called, 'Brahman', the God above all gods. Many people in the West think that Hindu's worship many different gods. That is not true."

Gavi explains that a Hindu may prefer a certain deity, but that deity simply represents one or more aspects of Brahman. He mentions a multitude of Hindu Gods and then returns to Brahman who is held above all. Brahma is the Creator, Vishnu is the preserver and Shiva the destroyer. These things I remember from my university class on world religions and in addition to my own hobby reading. I want to know what Gavi personally thinks of Karma.

I ask, "Gavi, what do you think brings good Karma?"

He answers slowly, "One must love not only those who are close to you but also those who are not. You should put others interests before yours, if you are able to. You must not hate. You must not be negative. You must worship the creator Brahma and all that has been created. Being alive should never leave your mind."

"That's what I thought Gavi. We know the same God." I state and make a cheers with him. He is glad that I understand him. We talk more about our respective cultures and experiences. It is all good.

Gavi looks at me writing notes on a scissors filters cardboard. He says, "I am going to be in your book. Say good things about our mutual God and me."

We are working on our third round of beers, yes, the double size ones. I do not think they come any smaller. "Thank you for stopping and having beer with me Gavi."

"Thank you Sir for the beer."

"I love beer."

"Me also. Must be careful not to have too much."

I laugh and say, "*YES, OTHERWISE PASSENGER DRIVE AUTO-RICKSHAW.*"

Gavi laughs and says, "Mr. Brent not drive. He has many beer before at Raj, he crash."

The sun inches into the horizon while we drive on a narrow road enclosed by palm and mango trees. The further we go the more difficult it is for Gavi to navigate. He is a good driver but he is not familiar with the area. He stops and asks directions a few times. I hear him say "Chikalamanil House" to a street vendor and the vendor points and says something in Malayalam. Finally, after leaving the bar twenty-five minutes ago, I recognize a familiar thin, winding road. Gavi honks the horn before steering through blind turns speeding along.

"Gavi, we are getting close." He slows down. I notice the pathway to the house. "*HERE. SEE PATH. CHIKALAMANIL HOUSE.*" We stop and I pay Gavi.

"No tip Mr. Brent. You bought beer."

I shake Gavi's hand, look him in the eye and say slowly, "You helped make my afternoon wedding party a success. Thank you very much Gavi for the talking and lessons on Hinduism and India. Take care of yourself and thank you for getting me home." I wish that hotel we just left was my home.

I walk up the path preparing to deal with any shit that I may get from anyone or everyone. Kavi knew what I was up to.

"Hi Kavi. How is married life?"

He shouts, "*WHAT THE HELL WERE YOU DOING? WERE YOU BAR HOPPING.*"

"*I WAS DRINKING WITH A HINDU AUTO-RICKSHAW DRIVER AT A NICE HOTEL DOWN THE ROAD. HE IS A GOOD HINDU WHO KNOWS HIS PRAYERS.*"

Kavi could not hold back the laughter. Kavi explains that Kuti made some phone calls and found out that one of his driver friends dropped me off at the Raj shortly after the reception. Someone went there to see if I was there around four o'clock and was told that I left in an auto-rickshaw. I never did get a chance to tell Kavi more about Gavi or meeting Biyar.

A few minutes later a friend of Kuti's drives up in a Landrover. It is the first one I have seen in India. The owner must have money. He gets out of the vehicle with his son. I am watching from the house between the air vent openings. Kuti hollers out, "Mr. Brent, come out please. There is someone I want you to meet."

I can tell that Kuti has something up his sleeve at my expense. I can hear it in his voice. I go out to the front drive and see a well-dressed Indian man about forty years old. He is standing on the other side of the hood of the rover and must have his son by the hand. I cannot see his son and his son cannot see me.

"Who would you like me to meet Kuti?"

"Oh, a friend of mine and his son."

"Hello Sir, my name is Brent."

He nods and like a dolt says nothing. He then brings his son around the side of the rover so that we are about four feet apart. His son screams bloody hell. He is one scared little boy. It is obvious that he has never seen white person before. After thirty seconds of high-pitched wailing, which brings everyone in the house to the front door to see what is going on, the boy's father explains to Kuti that the boy has never seen a white man in person. What a cruel joke to make on a young boy.

We are all at the table eating, thankfully not the little piranha fish. Kuti and Nogandichen are going on about something and laughing. I hear the word 'saipe' a few times. All of a sudden Pengal says loudly to Kuti and Nogandichen, "You should be ashamed at yourselves! You are sitting across from Brent who came all this way for his best friend's wedding and you are making fun of him in Malayalam. That is awful. It is more terrible to use that word. 'Saipe' is derogatory and racist. I dare you two to insult him in English!"

I know that they were joking about me but I did not realize it was as bad as Pengal sees it. I would never hit Nogandichen. He is an old man and my friend's father; Kuti is another story. He has been giving me a hard time all week. Kavi does not speak to my defense, perhaps because we are guests in his Uncle's house. Pengal lets it go after a little while and we finish our meal. Not wanting to sit around the table and talk I excuse myself, go to the riverbank and watch the moon reflect on the *Achen Kovil River*. It is easy to forgive and forget when you have the moon's watery reflection, life, love and Lalu to dwell on.

Free and on the Road

It is 6:45 a.m. and this guy is all packed raring to go to Cochin for the boat races. Kuti is ready too. Kavi and Phanni are late, which is not a surprise. I have known Kavi for many years. In those years I have never seen him be on time, except for his wedding. It has not been a big problem to deal with. When he is invited over or to set up a time to meet, one simply sets the time thirty minutes before the desired meeting time. If you want him to arrive at 7:00 p.m., I ask him to come at 6:30 p.m.. It is planned that Kavi and Phanni will spend the day at Phanni's relatives after visiting with Uncle George, Abraham and their families.

Kuti drives us, Kavi, Phanni, Nogandichen, Tarah, and I to Uncle George's place. We have breakfast and then I go over to visit with Abraham. I am so close to him in my heart. If I were an Indian there is no doubt that I would become his son-in-law. No chance though, I have a responsibility back home, a son that I hold so dear.

When I return next door, Uncle George gives me a hug and says, "Stay for awhile. There is no rush to leave."

I whisper, "Uncle George, if I had my way I would stay with you for another week, however, I need to move on and see India and her people. I also need to get away from Nogandichen. I will certainly miss you and your wife's cooking."

Uncle George, Nogandichen and I gather my rum and pack it in my suitcase. I give a bottle to Uncle George at Nogandichen's suggestion. After hugging Kavi goodbye and listening to last minute travel advice we say farewell to one another. I am in a rush for the boat races but one cannot rush the goodbyes as Tarah's family have been exceptionally good hosts.

The drive with Kuti is awesome so far. The scenery is different and more visible in the front passenger seat of a car. It is great to be alone and free on the road. The drive should take less than two hours. The only negative aspect is that Kuti keeps wanting so stop and have me try out some sort of cocoanut booze, called Hooti. It is a kind of cheap unprocessed killer alcohol. "Mr. Brent," he asks me, "Do you want to stop and try some Hooti? It is strong and very cheap." I am reminded of what Nogandichen lectured me before, "… do not drink or offer a drink with Kuti. He likes to drink too much." I think, to hell with you Nogandichen. You like to have a drink, why can't Kuti?

I pause, knowing that by the size of his beer gut and the fact that it did not contain any flab whatsoever cemented the advice that I had received earlier. He loves to drink.

"Next time Mr. Kuti, I want to get to Cochin so that I can see the dragon boats."

I know that we will not make the races on time. We stopped for too long to say our goodbyes on the way out. I do not allow myself to become upset as the great hospitality and lent wisdom of Uncle George prevails; patience, insight, wisdom, strong love and respect for Creation. I will remember him and treasure the time we had together for years to come.

"Kuti, what does it taste like?"

Staring at the broad palms containing full, voluptuous coconuts he says, "Bitter at first but better after the second one."

I figure the first one would likely have at least three to five ounces of strong alcohol. It could even be fifty per cent or a hundred-proof. "Do you get hung over if you tie one on with Hooti?"

"Tie what on?" he replies with his typical aggressive tone. He is so cock sure of himself. God love him, and so do I, but relax a little man. Have a drink, but not too much. There is no such thing as a happy dry alcoholic, just think of Hemmingway or Bukowski.

I reply in my best imitation of the Malayalam accent. "*DRINKING TO YOUR HEART IS SO CONTENT SO THAT YOU DO NOT WANT TO GO TO THE TEMPLE THE NEXT DAY.*" I am becoming quite good at saying, "*GO TO THE TEMPLE.*"

He laughs, then says with an unusual broad smile, "Fire."

As we drive I enjoy the scenery and analyze the radical drivers. The roads are somewhat crazy but Kuti is a good, fast driver. The highway is impressive compared to what I have seen earlier. It is almost as good as a Western double lane with ten-foot shoulders.

Looking through the tall palms, I search for animal life but only see shacks and people doing their laundry by hand in three foot buckets outside their home. Squeezing and twisting the fabric readying it for a clothes line or a large hot rock in the sun. Simplicity seems to bring about a certain joy. Reminds me of my mother doing laundry at the old house. Her putting pairs of pants through the ringer in the basement, then hauling the clothes upstairs and out to the back porch. Hanging them up and listening to the squeaking of the clothesline in the calm July air. A short poem comes to mind so I jot it down on a Scissors Filter package after unfolding it. I will call it 'Poor Man.'

A poor man happy for he has all his senses.
Wealthy man mad because he has to pay tax.
Even though the bastard cheats year after year.
And all this good man wants is a couple of beer.

The malaria pills are still giving me side-affects despite having stopped taking them days ago. I wish we could pull over and grab six beers. We have been driving for almost two hours. The cab fare that I am paying should include six or seven ice-cold beer on the house along with cooler, ice and two packs of cigarettes. Drink later. What the hell am I talking about? Damn pills.

As we pull into Cochin, Kuti announces, "Mr. Brent, it is just before one o'clock and we are in Cochin."

"Great!"

My back and neck are very sore from the taxi ride. They certainly do not make the taxis spacious here. The taxi is small. It is not quite as small as a Volkswagen bug. Anyone who is five foot seven or taller in the back seat has to crook their neck. Not a good time but nothing that some good stretching can't cure.

We are stopping at Mammea's to drop off one of my bags. A suit, shoes and other dress clothes will no longer be required. When Kuti is not looking I slip a bottle of rum out of my suitcase and hand it to Mammea. "This is for looking after my bag. I will pick it up later or Nogandichen can bring it back to Canada for me."

We get back in the cab and drive to the hostel. Kuti starts talking seriously, "Mr. Brent, I want to come to Canada. Do not tell my brother of this please. Not right away. You live in Canada and you are a lawyer. I need to find a way to come to Canada without my brother's help. He believes that I should stay here and look after our family house. I want to come to Canada. He brags about how it is so good in Canada. Then he makes bad on here, India. It is not fair."

"Life is not fair Kuti unless you get a hold of it and get rid of those who hold you back. Canada may not be for you. You will not be happy in Canada if you do not relax a little and love more. Regarding entrance to Canada, you require family support to come on a family visa. The only alternative is a business visa, which is extremely expensive. It is as much as a large house here. I will help you if you want but the answer is to be sponsored by your family that is in Canada."

"Thank you Mr. Brent."

"You are most welcome Sir."

It is New Years Eve. I check into the Y.M.C.A. hostel and am told that the dragon boat races occurred before noon. Well I know what to do, take another walk in good old Cochin. It is too late to get in touch with Matthew or Sammi so I will have a party by myself and read and write. On my way to downtown I walk by the field again. The children are not playing cricket today. The field is empty. The downtown is bustling. The traffic cop sits atop his podium pointing and blowing his whistle. He must be hot in that uniform.

I stop at a large store that stocks hardware. I walk right in and on the shelf to the immediate right of me, at eye level, is my little train ride savior;

a one-quart silver thermos. I pick it up at, shake it, note the price tag and walk over to the cash counter.

The clerk looks at the thermos and says, "One hundred twelve Rupees."

"*THAT IS A VEDDY GOOD PRICE.*"

He looks at me strangely so I smile, pay him and say, "I am practicing my Indian accent. No offence."

"I understand. I am just not used to a white person sounding like an Indian while using English. It is funny."

"*THANK YOU VEDDY MUCH SIR. I WILL BE ON MY WAY JUST NOW. YOU HAVE A NICE DAY.*"

I walk around town people watching and window-shopping. I stop at the dry goods store and buy ten packs of Scissors Filters and nine bottles of Pepsi. Kuti introduced me to his brand of cigarettes, Scissors Filters, after my Canadian Lights ran out. I will walk back to the hostel, drop off the purchases and go to the Hotel Empee for a few beers before settling down for the night in my room. I also must organize for the train tomorrow.

I enter the Hotel Empee. It is cool and almost empty of patrons inside. Most people must be with their family. It is a relaxing place to sit, write, drink beer and smoke. I am reminded of Dale back in Edmonton, always borrowing money from me. You know, if you lend a supposed friend five hundred dollars and you never see him again, you likely made a good investment.

It is early evening on New Years Eve and I am alone. I do not feel sorry for myself. Wonder why? I have five bottles of rum left and plenty of Pepsi sitting in the toilet tank keeping cool.

The rum and Pepsi is going down well. A bottle breaks, at least it was half empty. I am reminded of the no booze rule in the YMCA. I pour a stiff drink and then find myself searching for places to hide all this dough. The stack of paper Rupees is at least ten inches tall. Being told to put your cash in different places races through my buzzing mind. Life is good. Life is fabulous. Should I put most of the cash in socks? I decide to put the big bills next in the money belt, safety money in my socks and petty cash in my purse. Damn me to hell if I am wrong.

The room is all organized. The sun has set so I light a couple of candles. They are good company when you are enjoying your solitude, like a campfire. The flickering light casts shadows on the wall, keep ones eyes busy and mind at ease so you can think of your plans ahead. I want to develop my relationship with God and Creation more by learning more about nature's energy through India and her people.

I am having one of my best solo parties ever. No dancing though as I do not have any music.

Little did I know that the mosquitoes in Cochin like a white ass facing up … and attack.

I wake up late by not getting or more likely missing the wake up call. I am feeling somewhat bitten. I look in the mirror, "Those little bastards have poked me at least twenty seven times." Small red welts cover my ass, legs and back. Thank goodness I passed out on my front and prevented them from getting at my sausage. That would not be good if itchiness comes there. I curse, "You little buggers, how dare you take advantage of a drunken whitey after New Years Eve!"

I look at the clock. "Cripes almighty, it is 7:00 a.m.!" The train to Trivandrum leaves in forty-five minutes. Holy shit! I am just screwed. Fast shower. Fast hotel checkout. Fast cab. Late train. Right on!

The ticket clerk hands me a small piece of paper after I pay him seventy-five Rupees. That is a cheap trip, much cheaper than what I paid in Cochin. I put the paper in my pocket and find a place to sit. Grinning, looking up at the cloudless sky while sitting on the edge of the platform, I can barely contain my excitement. I am about to travel for the first time in my life without anyone holding me back. It is going to be legendary.

The train arrives. I look inside one of the cars at the back of the train. They are grungy and have wooden seats. I do not like them and am not too partial to some of the people inside them. Hmm. To hell with that let's try one of the cars more toward the middle of the train, I think. I walk up six or seven cars and look inside. No air conditioning but padded seats. This will do. I climb up and walk in.

Inside, a young India man is sitting on a single bench seat that faces inward. Across the aisle from him are sections of bench seats that seat three people. Each section has two benches facing one another. The design is not like train cars in the West where everyone faces forward and dwells silently on their dilemmas, instead of positively interacting with others. The booth type sections have seats midway up the wall and above, that fold down for sleeping. It is a comfortable setup.

I introduce myself to the young Indian man and ask if I can join him. He is a young university student named Raj who is in his first year of medicine. We have to sit cross-legged. Raj leans against a window that has quarter inch steel tubes that run horizontally across the window with three-inch gaps. The walls are a dusty white while the trim around the windows used to be blue. I sit leaning against a wall that serves as a partition from the other single booths.

Raj is on the shorter side and is quite thin but not gaunt. He is a handsome man except for the little ears that stick out some. He is dressed well and is friendly. He briefly tells me about himself and his family.

Raj asks me, "Now that the wedding is over what are you going to with your remaining three weeks in India?"

"I will travel and see as much of India as possible. I have met a few interesting people so far, such as a lawyer and a law student in Cochin, and hope to meet many more. In fact, I had beers the other day with an Hindu auto-rickshaw driver. We had a blast of a good time."

"That is interesting. What do you do for a living in Canada, Mr. Brent?"

"I am a lawyer."

"That makes meeting the lawyer and law student all the more interesting."

"For sure. I went to court with the lawyer and had lunch. The law student Sammi, who is taking his Master's in Law, took me out for dinner and we had a few drinks."

"India is treating you well so far."

"It certainly is. Raj, would you mind doing me a favor and call a friend to confirm that I am going to Cape Comorin or more properly called Kanyakumari?" I ask.

Raj replies, "I would not mind doing that at all. It would be my pleasure."

"Well thank you Raj. I will write the phone number down."

I hand him the piece of paper and pull out a roll of Rupees from my pocket. "No Brent, I will not take any money. Phone calls are not that expensive here."

"Okay. I would offer you some rum and Pepsi but it is too early for that."

He says, "I am getting off the train in about thirty minutes anyway. Now that I know that you have rum I would have gone to Kanyakumari with you. Which reminds me, I am impressed that you understand the importance of referring to places in India by their Indian name and not by some dry name given by the dry English such as Cape Comorin."

I reply, "One should always respect the country they are visiting. I love India."

"Brent, you are going to have a very good time in India with that attitude."

"For sure. Tell me more about medical school please." I ask.

We talk nonstop until the train comes to a halt. We shake hands before he departs at a small town which name I did not note. Raj is looking forward to spending a few days with his family.

The landscape is interesting. We pass villages situated sporadically along the tracks. Small homes and huts are nestled amongst coconut and banana groves. The train comes to a stop and Raj leaves. Time passes by as I marvel at the scenery. From town to plantation to village to grove to village and then another train stop. Wonderful colors, people and the sun shines on us all, including the Western Ghats mountain range that leads our way.

Sonny, his Father and Becoming a Swami

The train is rolling and clanking down the endless track. I discreetly reach into my carry bag and bring out a bottle of rum, pour a fifth of it into the thermos and top it off with Pepsi. I see a young Indian fellow watching me from across the aisle and three sections back. He is grinning and taking pleasure in watching the action. He looks to be about the same age as I. He seems to be a decent person even if he is wearing what looks like blue pajamas. He is sitting next to a large tough looking man who must be his father. The father has broad shoulders, dark hair and is balding. They are more fair-skinned than your average South Indian. They are probably from Northern India.

Directly across the aisle from me are two young pretty girls with their mother. The two girls are sitting across from each other, sharing a coconut with separate straws. It is a cute scene. They smile at the fact that I take their picture, as well as their mother. The girls are well behaved like many of the children that I have come across thus far.

The young man in the pajamas comes up and takes a seat beside me.

"Hello. My name is Sonny. I would like to meet with you." He does not have the accent but an accent, which is unique, something I have not heard before. His pronunciation is impeccable.

"My name is Brent. *WHAT THE HELL ARE YOU DOING HERE?*"

Sonny laughs, "Hey man, I see that you have been practicing the accent. You will be better understood here that way. You must slow down on the longer words if you use them. The answer to your question is that we are on a small father-son holiday to the Southern tip of India. Where are you going?"

"Do you know of this place called Kanyakumari? Apparently that is where this train ends and that is where I will start my travels."

"The place is also called Cape Comorin. It is a tourist site that honors a spiritual wondering monk named Swami. There is also a Ghandi museum there." Sunny states, while he glances at the thermos.

So the begging question is asked, "Sonny, would you like a rum and Pepsi?"

He says, "Yeah man." and delivers the head wiggle simultaneously—too cool.

We take our drinks and walk to an opening between the rail cars. I give Sonny a cigarette and light it. We talk and get to know each other's backgrounds. He knows Japanese fluently and has spent years in Japan being an interpreter. No wonder he speaks great English. He knows at least four languages.

Being concerned that I may have a bout of Malaria due to the mosquito bites I show Sonny the rash on my shoulders under my shirt. He states seriously, "It is the heat man. Don't show anyone. They will see you as sick and treat you as so, like you are low caste or even a leper."

"Okay Sonny, understood."

"Try to stay out of the direct sun for a few days, drink much water and try to stay cool. It will go away."

"I thought it might have had something to do with getting bit by so many mosquitoes last night. I must have been bitten at least twenty-five times." I say.

"You do not have malaria if that is what you are thinking. You would be really sick if you had malaria. The symptoms of malaria are high fever, headache, chills, shaking, stomach cramps and vomiting. It is like a severe flu man."

"Thanks for the information Sonny."

"Show me your train ticket please." I hand it to Sonny and ask why.

"I want to see if you have the correct ticket. See this, it says third class. You should be at the back of the train with the beggars and lepers." Sonny is trying hard to hold back the laugh. He continues, "Third class cars are the cheapest. They have wooden seats. You are lucky to be up here with us first class people man."

"That is okay. The conductors are small men and will not bother me."

"Okay tough guy, what brings you to India and this train?"

"I came to India for my best friends wedding in a small village called Pennukkara which is near Kottayam in Kerala. His name is Kavi. The wedding took place on December 29th and now my travels have started. I have been in India for almost two weeks now spending time with Kavi's family learning about India."

"Cool man. How long will you travel India for?" Sonny asks.

"Until the 24th of January."

"Do you have plans on what you may do?"

"After Kanyakumari, I want to go to Kovalam Beach for four or five days, then travel North, perhaps to Goa, Bombay and then Agra for the Taj Mahal. However, I am more interested in meeting people than seeing historical sites. I want to meet Muslims, Hindus, some Buddhists and learn about them and their faiths first-hand. Reading books is not enough."

"That is good so long as you do not spend more than three days in one place. You must call us up when you come to Bombay and stay with us. I can show you around. We are on a two week trip that started a few days ago."

"That is a nice offer Sonny. It may work out."

We spend the remainder of the train ride to Kanyakumari talking, joking and drinking rum and Pepsi, slowly, like gentlemen. No one notices, except Sonny's father.

Sonny and I are at the back of the coach having another cigarette. We are approaching one of the larger Western Ghats Mountains that we have seen so far. It is a glorious sight with arresting features. Grass meadows flow with a slight breeze over a berm, surrounded by tall palms on the left and a fruit grove on the right. The mountain is alone and somewhat flat on top. It has a bump on it towards the face that resembles a resting gigantic buffalo. What is most enticing to me, are the grasslands between the train and the stately palm trees. It is such a beautiful scene.

After taking a picture Sonny comments, "If your arm was still it will be a good picture. It is a great scenery man."

I reply, "Don't you mean that it is a great scene?"

"Fuck you man. You know what I mean!" I laugh and so does Sonny. *You know Keenan, if you choose to hang around with good company your life will be less stressful and more fun.*

We stop at a village shortly thereafter. While outside on a field, beside the train, Sonny sees two Japanese men, walks up to them and starts talking. It is entertaining to witness Sonny speak Japanese. I have no idea what Sonny is saying but one can surmise that it is about India. The Japanese fellows nod and smile. You can tell that they are happy to converse with an Indian in Japanese in India.

Sonny returns and says, "Did you see that? I was talking to them in Japanese. They do not know English so they were especially glad to talk with a Japanese Indian."

"Sonny that was very intriguing to watch. I liked how you guys bowed to each other when you were finished talking."

We return to our smoking area between the cars and travel on. Kanyakumari is not far off. The recently planted groves, only five feet in height, reach up to the sun. The red and brown mountain provides a good background. Sonny has left to talk to his father. I light a cigarette and take a sip of rum. Sonny returns and says, "When we get off the train my father says that you should come with us and he will find us the cheapest place to stay. It is not fancy hotel but a hostel. What do you think?"

"Sure, I would like your company. Just do not get fresh me with man."

Sonny says defensively, "I am not a fag man."

"I am kidding Sonny."

"I know but I do not like that kind of talk."

Saying seriously, "God loves gays or homosexuals just like everyone else and so do I. All I am saying is do not go grabbing my ass or something. Nothing against you, or Indian men in general, but you guys like to show your affection in sexual ways. Some men are not partial to that."

"You are really trying hard to be funny now. Get this straight; I like women; I like their bodies; I like to make love to women. I also like to drink with someone who has a brain."

"Sonny, I'll be your huckleberry."

"What does that mean?"

"It means that I like you and will support you like a brother, bro."

"That is good."

"Sonny, what is your father's name?

"Just call him Sonny Father. He does not speak English, only a few words."

"I like the sound of Sonny Father. It will work."

Sonny Father talks to a fellow at a desk and books two rooms at the hostel. We walk away and Sonny Father leads us to one door amongst many, along a building that is one story high, flat roofed, and long and rectangular. The exterior of the hostel is plain and uninviting.

The bed is actually a worn bench standing in the middle of the room. There is no running water or lighting. The door locks from the inside, which is a plus. One window ten inches wide and eighteen inches high graces the South wall. The unpainted dark concrete walls add to the dreary feeling of the room. This is definitely not economy class or even one star. It is the lowest class or star you could have, not even close to half a star. But you know what? I like it. It fits the situation and it is almost free. Sonny Father did not hand over too many Rupees to the room clerk. One only has to sleep here—might just have to have an extra drink or two for a good night's sleep. The bathroom and showers are a two minute walk away which have plenty of water and they are clean.

Standing in the shade outside of the room waiting to meet Sonny and his father, I watch two young boys play ball with their fathers. Large stately trees grace the hostels grounds. I think of my son Keenan. I can't wait to play football with him and teach him how to box. I may not be that great of a boxer but I can sure take the hits. I like being punched in the head so long as I get the chance to punch back. The thump and split second flash of light running through one's head is thrilling. Makes me crazy. I like it. Reminds me of an old high school friend named Ron Nolan who played for the Melville Millionaires. Not only could he fight, he relished the adrenalin rushes of being punched and fighting back.

Sonny and his father exit their room. We are walking along a path leading to the ocean when we come upon a statue of a youngish man in a turban, not a Sikh turban, but similar and loosely fitting. He looks stoic, strong and serious. You can see in his face that he is a thinker. We stop and look up at him.

Sonny turns to me, "This is the Swami, Swami Vivekananda. The true Swami. He traveled much of India on a spiritual quest. Just like you, a true swami, swami."

"Well, thank you Sonny. It is an honor to be called a swami."

Sonny Father looks amused. He chuckles and says like a Sergeant, "swami", and then points toward the ocean and then leads the way.

Sonny explains, "This is where the three oceans meet. The Bay of Bengal, the Indian Ocean and the Arabian Sea."

"Wow!"

Sonny goes on, "See the different colors, mixing together, blue and green."

"Yes Sonny. I want to have a quick swim. If I don't do it now I never will. Take my camera please."

I walk down the rocks under the watchful eyes of Sonny Father and Sonny.

"Be careful swami." Sonny advises.

"Please tell your father I will be careful not to fall." Sonny Father has not spoken a full sentence of English yet. He is probably saving it.

"Hey. Look out for all that shit man. Look at all the shit!" Sonny exclaims.

The sun is setting. I must move quickly as the return walk up will be twice as hard. The rocks are sharp and have mounds of seagull and other types of bird poop spread over the flat parts. The water is cool. Sonny is on the rocks. He waves. I pose for a picture and Sonny moves a few yards closer. Big waves are coming in. One smacks me against a large boulder. Time to leave.

There are loads of Indian tourists here to see the sunset. Sonny points out toward a small island and says, "That is the Swami Memorial Rock over there. We will go visit that place and you can learn about the Swami." The rock is about a half a kilometer from shore.

"Yes. That will be good. I have heard of Swami before and want to learn more about him."

Sonny is enthusiastic in saying, "You will learn so much about the Swami here man you will become a real fucking Swami. Because you man are a natural Swami."

I reply, "Right on brother!" and I smack him with a right fist square on the upper arm.

"Is that how you Canadians say thank you?" Sonny asks while rubbing his arm.

"Not exactly. That is how a brother says thank you. But not too hard. It is better than holding your buddy's hand or patting his rear end." I explain.

"What are you talking about? I do not hold a man's hand or pat his rear end. Are you trying to get me going?"

"No, but I have seen many men holding hands while walking down the street in Cochin. And my buddy Kavi used to pat me on the rear end on a Friday night after a few beers."

Sonny finishes the topic by stating, "That does not mean that it is part of our culture. We say thank you, nod our heads and smile for thank you. If a person is a very close friend we may hug them. That is all."

It is morning and Sonny and I chase a peacock around in the compound while we wait for Sonny Father. Sonny says, "My dad has a full day planned. No rum until after dark. I promised him."

"No problem Sonny. I do not like to drink during the day unless you are on a beach or at a golf course. When on tour it is good to drink water. An afternoon beer or two at an air-conditioned pub during the tour is always nice. However, since Sonny Father no longer drinks it will be respected."

"Good man. Oh, there is Sonny Father swami. I am hungry."

We have breakfast at the cafeteria. Sonny Father pays.

Sonny Father hires a cab for the day and we go on tour. Our first stop is a tall Hindu temple about eleven stories high. It is rectangular and narrows with each story. It is made of rock and is carved full of Hindu deities. It is dimly lit and cool inside. The floor is stone with much sand on it. Sonny dips his finger in some red dye at the foot of a deity, that looks like a variation of Ganesh, and touches his forehead. He does the same to me and says, "Now you are a Hindu like the Swami man." We continue to explore every square foot of the temple on the main floor. Only the monks are allowed to enter the upper levels. There are many Hindu pilgrims inside praying to the different deities. The pilgrims are wearing bright orange robes. A group of temple monks are playing drums and ringing bells in a circle.

Sonny Father takes his time at each station. He is standing before the deity of Shiva. The carving of Shiva is a little short of being three feet tall. She stands on a shelf that is inlaid into the stone wall. This particular Shiva, takes the form of both man and woman. Her right chest is that of a man and she has a breast on her left. She wears a crown (I refer to her as a she because she has a boobie—we do not know the rest of her anatomy) and has four arms. Her waist is thin and hips round. She has a nice figure. Shiva is an important manifestation of one aspect of the main God, Bhrama. Many people think Hinduism is polytheistic or that Hindu's worship many Gods and are therefore bloody heathens. That is not true. Like native culture and native religions in the America's, the focus is on the Creator and worship is made to the different gifts that the Creator has given mankind. Rain, fire and the promise of a good afterlife. Shiva destroys evil and protects those who are good. It is fabulous to be here just now—I am reminded of the different Hindu deities learned in our World Religions class before law school. This particular Shiva is something to look at as she is quite feminine.

Sonny walks up to us and says, "Hey man. This Shiva has only one breast. This is the half-man half-woman Shiva. What do you think is below swami?"

"I am not quite sure Sonny. Because of the shapely hourglass figure one would expect a vagina. A Darwinist would expect a hermaphrodite."

"What the hell is a Darwinist? I know hermaphrodite but a Darwinist? Is he some kind of prophet?"

"Darwinists are usually atheist and adhere to the principles of Charles Darwin and his theories of evolution."

Sonny responds by scratching his chin and saying, "Oh, those fuckers who believe in the Big Bang and all that bullshit."

"You got it Sonny."

Outside on the street we walk up to a mobile Hindu temple or shrine with colorful four-foot deities of Shiva and Ganesh standing guard on top. The shrine has ten-foot high wheels made of wood with it's axles being supported by rocks. There is a monk on the very top working. This thing is big. It has to be at least forty feet high, thirty feet across and twice as long. A man is dwarfed as he poses for a picture standing next to a wheel. We agree that the shrine must be used for parades and festivals.

After lunch at the cafeteria, Sonny Father does not let me pay for the group or myself. He also buys the taxi driver lunch. The food is served on round tin trays that have different sized divisions or bowls that separate the meat, rice, vegetables and sauces. A good lunch runs less than two dollars. The food is basic, healthy and it tastes very good. If you do not like curry India it is not for you.

Sonny Father, Sonny and I are in a long queue to catch a boat to what some people call, Swami's Rock. It is home to the Swami Memorial for the great Swami Vivekananda. Some young guys jump the queue. Sonny calls out, "Hey man. That's not fair!"

I join in, "*WHAT THE HELL ARE YOU DOING? BE POLITE, NOT ASSHOLE. GO TO THE TEMPLE AND SAY YOUR PRAYERS.*" We laugh hard, acting like crazy brothers that no one would mess around with. Sonny Father is grinning; he is starting to loosen up.

As the boat moves closer to Vivekananda Rock, it becomes clear that the Swami impressed many people; making enough of an impression to warrant the building of a majestic temple and memorial. Almost all of the rock surface above water is utilized. A large part of the tiny island's rock face is faded white, adorned by a orange triangular flag.

As we leave the boat and walk up the aisle way, Sonny gives me a short introduction. "Swami was a very important spiritual leader. After touring India and spreading the word of unity and tolerance amongst the religions he ended up here. He swam out to the rock and contemplated his next move. You will learn a lot about him inside."

Once inside the shrine itself, more detailed information is offered. Swami Vivekananda was born with the name Narendranath Datta. He became 'Swami' later on after much study as a Hindu monk. He spent time in a temple in Varanasi, which is supposed to be a very holy city in Calcutta. Barefoot and penniless, the Swami travels to Agra trying to find his path amidst God and conflicting religions.

Swami rebukes the caste system after an 'untouchable' refuses to share a smoke from his pipe. He walks away after being refused and thinks of the terrible caste system and decides to rebuke it. He returns to the untouchable and convinces him to share a smoke.

Swami wandered India as a monk initially begging for his food or money to buy his dinner. He did much walking, all the time thinking and praying. He was on a mission to discover more in God, in himself and his countrymen. He saw spiritual vigor even in the very poor and stuck up for them. I read that Swami goes to a railway station in Hathras, Bengal. The stationmaster, named Surat, was fascinated by Swami's stature and looks. He approaches him and invites Swami for lunch. After an intense exchange of ideas they become friends. Surat later becomes a disciple of the Swami.

Swami received a mission from his guru, Sri Ramakrishna, before he left on his travels; to serve man as God would. Swami tells Surat that he must rejuvenate India so that it becomes dynamic again. He describes a need for great India to earn the respect of the world through her spiritual power. Surat follows Swami for the next leg of the journey. After returning to his former temple for a short while, Baranogore Math, Swami leaves Calcutta and heads to Northern India vowing not to return until fully self-realized. It is July, 1890.

Swami was a very well spoken man. The Maharaja Ajit Singh of Khetri at Mount Abu became a disciple after hearing Swami's words.

Swami Vivekananda is an impressive figure. We think alike. I have long thought that there must be unity and tolerance, and most importantly—Love, amongst world religions, if man's world is to be a better place. It is totally easy to agree with him in that in order to become wise and strong one must first understand the knowledge that God's presence is within you. I would add, God is energy; energy can be harnessed by those who know God. To know God is to Love.

Swami meets important people, both secular and religious, on his way to South India. Once he reaches Kanyakumari, he is a popular figure with many people awaiting his arrival. A number of people encourage him and offer financial support. Swami decides to accept an offer to go to the Parliament of Religions in Chicago. This conference was brought about because Chicago was hosting the World Fair.

Swami takes a ship to Vancouver and lands there on July 25, 1893. Once at the Chicago conference the Swami wows the crowd. He captures the hearts and minds of those in attendance and those who read about his famous address. He receives a standing ovation as soon as he finishes speaking these famous, simple, opening words, "Brothers and sisters of America …".

After reading almost everything there is to read I go to the deck to have a cigarette, reflect and take some notes. Sonny left me alone once he realized that I was into Swami. We will learn more about Swami later.

It is overcast, windy and much cooler. It feels great to cool off. No lungis here, all long pants and a white guy wearing shorts. A dark cloud is blowing in from the South. We may get a storm. The expansive red deck circling the outer edge of the rock contrasts the darkening sky and the deep blue-green ocean.

We return to the hostel cafeteria for dinner and order Thali meals again. A Thali meal usually consists of coconut chutney, rice, chickpeas, curd yogurt and chapati bread. Thali is a Hindi term for plate. Sonny and his father are Hindi. We walk up to the serving line with Sonny Father leading the way. The server knows I like the vegetable curry and mounds the largest compartment in the round tray with it. The next compartment is filled with rice. There is also curd or yogurt, chutney and awful chickpeas. They are refused as they are bland and do not hold the spice. Chappattis are a form of bread and two thins ones do the trick. One could eat the Thali meal twice a day if chicken curry is available.

The meal is good and goes down fast. Again Sonny Father does not let me pay for us or myself. Sonny and I sneak away in search for a place to have a few drinks after walking back to the hostel. We find a small stand up bar that has a dirt floor. An old man comes in and pays for a mickey of rum. He opens the cap and downs the bottle. He exhales and walks out with a smile. Sonny tells me of his childhood and future dreams. We share many stories of growing up and some memorable life events.

Sonny says, "You know swami. I am glad that I called you swami, because you are a real swami. No show and all glow." Sonny laughs hard and I do not know if I should take him seriously. "It is true. You are a true swami. The way I meet you on the train. The way you act. Your generosity and the way you deal with people. I also see spirit in you and you share your rum."

"Thank you Sonny. You are a good man. You know what time it is."

"Let's go somewhere else. We have been here for more than an hour. Let's have a drink at the hostel on the bench."

"Okay Sonny, let's do it. It should not be a problem as long as we do not get too loud. We need to get some Pepsi."

"I know where to go. We passed a store on the way here." says Sonny.

We arrive at the store. The typical hot dog stand type, without the hotdogs. The ware is similar to our corner stores but without frozen or fresh food. There are two young men in their early twenties sharing a cigarette. I go up and ask for a large bottle of Pepsi. I ask, "How much is it?" as one of the vendors places the bottle on the high counter.

"Forty Rupees."

I pay him. Sonny is on the road out of earshot. I walk to him. Sonny asks, "How much did he charge you?"

"Forty Rupees."

"Forty Rupees! Look on the bottle man! It says eighteen Rupees. Let's go talk to him, better yet, you make him give you the twenty-two Rupees he stole from you. You need to learn not to be taken advantage of."

So I walk up to the vendor and his buddy and give it my best Apu style, *"EXCUSE ME SIR. LOOK AT THE BOTTLE SIR, HERE."* I point to the price on the bottom edge of the bottle. *"IT READS EIGHTEEN RUPEES, NOT FORTY. YOU OWE ME TWENTY RUPEES. PAY ME NOW!"*

I look up at his puzzled face as he reaches into his pocket and say, *"YOU NEED TO GO TO THE TEMPLE AND SAY YOUR PRAYERS. JUST BECAUSE OF MY SKIN IS WHITE DOES NOT MEAN THAT I AM GREEN IN INDIA. SHAME ON YOU SIR! YOU ARE A BAD MAN. WHERE IS YOUR CONSCIENCE?"*

Sonny is grinning so hard it looks like that he may crap as he holds his stomach. He rights himself and states, "swami, I think you scared that guy. He thought you were so mad you were going to beat him."

"Yes. I sure had him going. Acting classes paid off again. Thanks for the advice and direction."

On our way to the hostel, Sonny caps the lesson by relating a classic Swami Vivekananda story that can be characterized as a Jesus parable. "Even a Swami has to stand his ground and be tough at times man!" He goes on to describe Swami on a train. "Swami V. is on a train. Across from him are two well to do Englishman who think that they own the place. They cut Swami down in English thinking he does not know the language. They laugh to each other calling him a vagabond and a dirty beggar. A short time later Swami orders a tea in English. They ask him why he did not react to their offences earlier. Swami tells them, 'This is not the first time that I have met fools.'"

"That is a good story. It takes balls and wit to come up with that line Sonny."

Sonny replies, "Like you swami. You are aware, like Columbo."

We get a bottle of rum from my room and two glasses. We are set for some Indian cocktails. Sonny asks, "If I come to Canada can I stay with you?"

"Sonny, for as long as you want, until I am no longer a bachelor."

Sonny pipes up, "I am serious man! I will be coming to see you."

"Sonny, I am also serious. I do not bullshit unless I give a hint that I am doing so, such as a grin. On a serious note, if you stay for more than two weeks I will have to put you to work."

He says, "Work? Work? I do not do physical labor you fucker!"

"I bet you don't do dishes or cook either, you spoiled shit. I run a law office. You can do couriers, such as making bank deposits, delivering letters and buying stationary. Things to keep you busy when I am at work during the day. Then you feel good about your extended stay and I feel good that you are pulling your weight."

"That is good swami. Then maybe I could stay long enough to find a Canadian wife and stay for good."

"Be my guest Sonny. I will help you if you wish. Canada may seem to be an answer for many, however, as you may have heard, the grass is always greener on the other side of the fence." Sonny looks puzzled so I explain further. "A little puppy dog is walking along a stream. He has a bone in his mouth that he found a day before. It was fresh then but not so much now. He walks up to the bank of the stream. He sees his reflection but thinks it is another puppy with a good bone. He snaps down opening his mouth to grab the bone and loses his. Now he has no bone."

Sonny looks at me and says, "Hey man, I am no puppy. I am a lion. I can handle the West." It is getting late. We hear a familiar gruff voice coming from the dark.

"Gentleman."

We say nothing.

Sonny Father speaks louder, "Gentleman."

I nudge Sonny and he tells Sonny Father that we will be finished soon and then whispers to me, "We are grown men. We can take care of ourselves." He confides further, "He has lived his life, now he should let me live mine."

"Sonny, that is a harsh thing to say. You should not repeat that to your father. He has not fully lived his life and he has not finished with caring about you. He will care for you as long as he is alive. Furthermore, maybe he is concerned with us getting picked up for public drinking even though we are acting like gentlemen."

Sonny nods. "Let's have one more drink, like gentlemen."

We are outside the hostel rooms and the morning sun beats down on us, casting crisp shadows. Sonny looks good dressed in all black. Black pants are far more manly than the blue pajamas. Sonny Father is wearing black pants, a long sleeved blue shirt and a matching black baseball cap with a red trimmed brim. I, again, am dressed like a beach bum. Sonny Father has a few sites in mind to visit. I think he has done his research.

The temple has a courtyard full of vendors. So far, Sonny Father has not let me spend a single Rupee. I want to buy a large wooden elephant. Sonny says to me, "I will get father's attention and keep him distracted from you. He has been watching over you more than he rides me the last two days."

We are walking along one of the main streets in town when Sonny Father notices the bag swaying in my left hand. "What did you buy Mr. Gentleman?" He likes to call me Mr. Gentleman. I show him the elephant. He looks at the price tag and nods yes. I am relieved as he is pleased.

Our cab slowly navigates sharp turns as it climbs a narrow road to a small plateau on the side of the mountain. The cab can only take us so far. We park at a small area just large enough to turn around and park a couple of cars. The steps carved into the side of the slope are small and many. Fifteen minutes later we reach a temple. The temple is small yet appreciating. What I thought was going to be a Hindu temple turns out to be a small Catholic Church. We walk in and feel taken. There is nothing here worth looking at inside. No problem as the vantage point from up here is great.

"Sonny, I think I should leave tomorrow and go to Kovalam Beach. I want a nice place to sleep, drink some beer on the beach and swim in the ocean everyday. I think we have seen most of what there is to see here." I say.

Sonny walks over to his father, speaks with him and then returns. "Father says that we will go to the Ghandi museum and you can buy some books written by Ghandi. Then we will go to the Swami Exhibition and then to the bus station so you can buy a ticket to Kovalam Beach. Sound Good?"

"*VEDDY GOOD MAN.*"

The permanent photo exhibition for Swami Vivekananda is large and brightly inviting. Again, Sonny Father will not let any Rupees leave my wallet. We go in and I stop at a wall that has a map of the exhibition. There are forty-one different stations with pictures and accounts of Swami. I read every one of them. After reading thirteen stations I begin to wonder if Swami had a masculine side to him, that is, enjoying female company. Two stations later I come to a photo of Swami surrounded by three pretty ladies. Even though it could have been a Chicago photo opportunity, the smile on his face answers my question.

I learn that Swami studied the life and teachings of Jesus, Mohammed and Buddha. It is fascinating reading. Swami has a strong message of unity among the major religions in India, Hinduism, Islam, Sikhism, Buddhism and Christianity.

Swami understood the suffering of the exploited poor at the hands of British rule. It is also pleasing that he talks of the dark aspects of ignorance, like the two Englishmen on the train. The Exhibit is exciting and leaves one hoping that the Swami had a really good time in Chicago. He certainly deserved so.

Inside the bus station I am persistent in being assured that it is an express bus to Kovalam Beach. At least Sonny Father let me pay for my own ticket. I am told that it is a one and a half hour ride with very few stops. I do not like the bus, any bus. People do not seem to behave on the bus. Taking the bus can be like shopping at a Wal-Mart on a Saturday morning. It is crowded and people are rude.

Perhaps Sonny Father thinks that Sonny and swami should spend some time apart as he is more than happy to have our taxi guide to take us to the station to buy the bus ticket. Sonny whispers that he will make sure to convince his dad to take him to Kovalam Beach and meet up with me a few days later.

Sonny Father may be a bit of a hard ass but he is a man's man. He finds a good place to eat and sticks with it. He plans our trips around the cafeteria and meal times. We have lunch and dinners here without variation. The food is good, why take a chance on something different and pay eight times the cost for something that may be inferior?

Outside the cafeteria I say, "Sonny Father, I thank you for everything. Once again dinner was very good." Sonny Father nods his head. I reach out and shake his hand.

He shows his soft side and pleasantly says to me, "Gentleman swami."

"Sonny, I hope that your father understands how much I appreciate his generosity and hospitality. He has taken me under his wing and taught me to be frugal. You also with the Pepsi incident."

"He does swami. I can see through your actions that you appreciate kind things done for you and so can my father. Let's go out for a walk after we go back and I will explain to father what we are doing. We can have a bottle of your rum and I will buy the Pepsi."

"Sounds good to me Sonny." I answer.

Sonny and I are walking down the main street in Kanyakumari, drinking our rum and Pepsi out of large plastic Pepsi bottles. It is a good thing that I have saved two of them. They are sure turning out to be handy just now. We take a seat on a bench and watch the tourists walk by. I say, "Sonny, do you still have my business card?"

"Yes I do. I am coming to Edmonton to see you fucker! You had better feed me good too!"

"WHAT THE HELL SONNY. YOU COME TO EDMONTON AND I WILL FEED YOU REAL GOOD. YOU WILL HAVE TO WASH THE DISHES AND I WILL MAKE THE CHICKEN CURRY."

"I am sure that we will have a good time." Sonny says. We walk over to the point and sit down on some rocks. The stars are brilliant tonight. There is little wind. We talk of the future.

Express-bus my ass. We keep stopping and the driver and bus conductor guy keeps packing more people into the bus. I am asked to put my suitcase on my lap. We stop again and I put the suitcase on the overhead luggage rack. A fat Indian squeezes between another passenger to my left and me. We bounce along the bumpy road.

"Burp" goes the fat guy. I cannot believe that he just belched so loudly. He does not even cover his mouth! A few minutes pass by. Fat guy turns his head in my direction and burps again! It smells.

"*WHAT THE HELL ARE YOU DOING SIR! YOU ARE A PIG, DIRTY, DIRTY. PLEASE DO NOT DO THAT AGAIN.*" People are looking at us. I figure that he does not understand what I have just said but at least he gets the gist that I am upset. Do not travel by bus here unless you absolutely have to.

We are approaching Kovalam Beach and fat guy gets off the bus. What a relief. Now I can breathe and enjoy the scenery. It is exciting to be traveling solo, to be full of life and open to whatever may occur.

Kovalam Beach

Kovalam Beach, is a place where life is going to become quite interesting. I get off the bus, stretch and wink at the sky. I see a dark Indian with a mischievous grin. He asks me if I have a room booked. Looking cautiously, I nod no and take note of him. He looks like a party guy as his eyes are bloodshot from the night before. The business card he hands me, in an assertive yet pleasant manner, reads: Hotel Lekshmi Nivas, Light House Beach, Kovalam. Trivandrum, Kerala, South India. For Bath Attached Room. K. Vidyadharan. It is easy for him to see that I need a room being a white tourist right off a bus. The business card is professional so I let my guard down and smile.

"My name is Kumar. Would you like to look at a room?" He grabs my bags after I agree to check out the place.

The room is great. It has two single beds with clean sheets and blankets. The floor and walls are clean. The door is blue and so is the window trim. It is a smaller motel with only four rooms. A small set up but it will work out great because there is a vendor that sells Pepsi, cigarettes, water and other necessities at the West end of the mini hotel. It is an Austin Mini hotel and very groovy.

Kumar excuses himself for a few minutes. He returns with two ice-cold beers, yes the twenty-four ounce kind. We enjoy our beer while Kumar explains the cost of the room and advises that the register can be signed tomorrow. The room is going to cost about eight dollars Canadian per night. The best room for my dollar ever.

"Mr. swami, do you like to smoke?" Kumar asks while grinning big time.

"Yes, I like to smoke when at the beach."

"Do you want this much?" He cups his hands.

"Yes. How many Rupees?"

"Five hundred."

"That is okay."

Kumar does the head wiggle, downs his beer and leaves.

There is not too much to unpack. While setting out simple things such as my shaving kit, books and notepads, my thoughts turn to marijuana. How does one justify to his own son, that his father likes to smoke it on certain occasions, even though it is against the law to possess it in most jurisdictions. It is people who are so wound up and uptight that are against smoking pot or tolerating other people who smoke pot. They are the ones who really need to have a puff.

Keenan, I have only a few rules about drugs. Do not do any drug beyond marijuana. You can become addicted to hard drugs very fast. Even though I have never done heroin, ecstasy, meth or crack cocaine, I do not have to in order to see if they are good or not. They are very bad because they kill people and make you crazy.

If you smoke marijuana, please do not get into it until you have successfully completed your first year of university. Do not smoke a lot of it either. Use it as a treat on a Friday night. Do not associate with people who do other drugs. People who sell and produce hard drugs do not care about others, only them-selves. These people are evil. Marijuana is different. It grows naturally, and naturally man has been smoking it for thousands of years. Perhaps Jesus smoked it when he visited India in his twenties. I am not encouraging you to smoke marijuana Keenan. As your father, I prefer that you do not smoke any-thing, except the odd cigar as an adult. Am I a hypocrite for preaching 'do as I say and not as I do?' The answer is no kid as I am a little crazy and you are not.

Do not let yourself stand in the way of your own destiny. If you are not where you want to be, get off your ass and take yourself there. Do not let any-one else hold you back. Befriend good people only Keenan. Bad people have bad Karma. You do not want bad Karma. Good friends make positive influences and this helps you make good decisions during your life. Good character is almost everything—add some love and it is.

There is a knock at the door. It is Kumar beaming away. He says me, "Be careful where you smoke it. Do not smoke it on the beach during the day unless you go out into the water. The police will not put you in jail but they will want a bribe. It will cost you a hundred dollars American."

"I understand Kumar. Thank you." I then ask Kumar to roll one. It is prudent to make sure that he is a smoker and not setting me up. It is not a strong possibility as he is an agent for the owner of a small beach hotel. Setting me up for a fall would really hurt the reputation of Hotel Lakshmi. Kumar finishes rolling a fat one.

We finish a second round of beer and I pay Kumar for the smoke. He tells me to pay the manager directly for the room tomorrow afternoon. He says good night, leaves and is not seen again.

After I finish settling in I decide to find a restaurant. Once outside the door and through the small patio, it is a fifteen second walk to the beach and less than a minute to the ocean. Kovalam Beach is on the Western coast of India and is a one hour drive North of Trivantrum. This is a big tourist destination for Europeans with a decent selection of beach restaurants.

The first restaurant I come upon is called the Velvet Dawn. There is no one seated here. Looking up to the raised beach patio I see a frowning middle aged Indian lurking about. He sees me look down at three fish, illuminated by candlelight, on a table at beach level. I ignore his pleas to buy his fish and walk away. Fish that have been sitting out for a long time can be dangerous.

There are a few tourists speckled along various raised restaurant patios. A sign at a large restaurant reads Santana's. Well that has to be a good place to have a beer and listen to good music. Stepping up from the beach onto the wooden raised deck takes some concentration. The deck is large and the steps are not your usual seven inch risers but ten inch risers. There is a row of high back wooden chairs, the kind that you sink into, lining the front edge of the patio facing the ocean. They lean back and wide, large, flat armrests leave plenty of room to hold an ashtray and a beer.

I choose one of the chairs in the middle. There is only one other guest here, a woman seated four chairs to the South. After I receive my beer and pay, she looks over and asks me to join her, "Excuse me, would you like some company?" Her accent is definitely German.

"Sure." I get up and sit in a chair next to her.

"Hello, my name is Edith. Thank you for joining me. What is your name?"

"My name is Brent Bittner, however, while in Kanyakumari or Cape Comorin a man gave me the name swami, after a wonderful Hindu monk named Swami Vivekananda."

"Brent is nice but swami has a ring to it and sounds Indian, swami."

She asks me what brings me to India and to Kovalam Beach. I give her a short version. I do not like to talk too much when I first meet a person. I like to hear more about them. There is a time and place to entertain with stories.

"What brings you to Kovalam Beach Edith?"

"I come for the winters and I have been doing it for years. I come in the fall and leave in the spring. I am divorced from a wealthy German lawyer. I enjoy the beach here and meet many interesting people."

Edith is pleasant and forward. Her long brown hair has soft curls flowing down to the ends. She is around fifty years old. Her face is pretty and she has an enticing smile. She is a little heavy but carries herself quiet well. She is voluptuous and has a sexy figure. I feel good about meeting her and it is not sexual.

I ask her, "Is the weather good here during the winter months Edith?"

"Most of the time the weather is just right. It cools down at night especially after a cloudy day." She pauses and continues, "I am waiting for my friend Harry. We are going to eat at one of the beach restaurants. Do you want to join us?"

"Certainly. Thank you for the invitation. I truly appreciate it because once I unpacked and settled in, it was dark outside. I have no idea where to eat."

"Well you ran into the right lady. I know almost everything there is to know about this place. It is my second home. My friend Harry is a local and grew up in this area."

Harry arrives and Edith introduces us. I look him in the eyes and shake his hand with a regular grip, not trying to cause discomfort and prove how strong I am. *Keenan, shaking the hand of another man properly is such a very important attribute. First impressions are very important. Remember Keenan, you never get a second chance to make a first impression. You look him in the eyes, smile genuinely like you are meeting a best friend for the first time. It is not a task at all if you are one with yourself and exude joy.*

We order three beers and talk. Harry is a masseuse and appears to be Edith's lover. He is about twenty-five years old. A good looking man with a medium build. His dark eyes are serious and penetrating. His hair is of medium length with moderate curls. Harry does not warm up to me right away. He is just being a cautious good man. Can't trust too many men around your woman. Many men think through their sausages and not their heads and hearts.

Harry asks me, "What do you do for a living in Canada swami?"

"I am a lawyer."

"What kind of lawyer?" asks Edith.

"An honest one."

"That is funny man." says Harry.

"What kind of law do you practice?" Edith asks.

"Litigation, contract law, real estate law, wills. I try to stay away from criminal law as I do not like criminals and I stay away from family law as the lawyers and clients tend to be high strung."

"What do you do Harry?" I ask.

"I am a masseuse."

"No wonder Edith is with you. I bet you are good at it because you look strong."

"I think so. What do you think Edith?"

"Yes Harry, you are a good masseuse and a strong man."

Harry asks me, "Where are you staying swami?"

"At the Hotel Lekshmi."

"You are my neighbor swami." Says Edith. "If you walk out your door walk toward the beach and jump over the brick wall adjacent to the vendor's stand, take thirty steps you will be at my door."

Harry says, "Honey, did you have to give swami directions to your room so soon." We laugh.

The remainder of the evening turns out swell. It is fabulous to meet decent people that are helpful and fun to be with. I could not have met a better couple on this beach.

I wake up early around seven in the morning. It is a good time to place telephone calls. I call Keenan first and receive a message to call to my mother's home in Melville, Saskatchewan.

"Hello."

"Mom, it's Butch." She likes me to refer to my old nickname that was suggested by my mother's friend and babysitter soon after I was born.

"Your father has taken a turn for the worse. He has been in the hospital for a few days and it does not look like he is going to come out."

"Should I come home?"

"If you can do it easily and if it will not cost you a lot of money. Keep in mind that you were just here in October."

"That is the reason why Keenan and I came to Melville, to give Keenan a memory of his grandfather and for us to say hello and hug dad. I knew that dad would get worse and die while I was in India. That is the reason why we came, to say our goodbyes without saying them."

"I understand. Don't feel bad if you decide not to come home."

"Even if I do mom, it is so close to the new year, I do not know about the flights. Plus I have to get to Melville from Edmonton. There is no way I could change the carrier for the flight over the ocean. Lastly, it could take three to four days to get home. Let me think about it and I will call you back. Goodbye mother. I love you. Give Father my best."

"I love you too son. Be careful there."

"I will mom. Bye."

Shit! I knew this would happen but I will not let myself feel guilty for not returning. Dad would understand. I am not in a financial position to get home in a rush either. Cripes I had to borrow money from Kavi just in case I run short at the end of the trip. Lastly and more importantly, I do not want to mourn my father's impending passing with any of my siblings. I would rather mourn alone. I decide to walk the beach and think.

An hour later I return to Edith's hotel and ask for the phone again. I decide to stay put in Kovalam Beach and call home often. I call mom and tell her that it would be very difficult, if not impossible, to get home within a few days. I told her that I could not afford it either. Hell, I don't even have a credit card with me.

"I will let your father know."

"Thank you mom."

"Don't feel guilty Butch. You saw your dad in October with Keenan. You have invested a lot in your trip so go and enjoy yourself." Good words from a smart lady. "Goodbye my good son. Call home in a few days."

"I will mother. I love you."

"I love you too. Bye."

I go for a two hour walk along the beach and think things over some more. Dad got lung cancer two years ago. They took a third of his lung out. The scar was still fresh when he and mom came up to see me called to the bar or be sworn in as a lawyer.

The operation seemed to work, but a year later they found cancer in the lymph nodes in his neck. The doctors had given him a year to live. Once you get lymphatic cancer you are usually screwed. I know that from nursing school. I will stay on here for a week and not feel guilty about it.

If father knew how this trip is affecting me spiritually he would not want me to leave. So I turn my thoughts elsewhere and away from the negative and walk on. The stress from Western life has virtually vanished. India does seem magical, like a magic carpet ride. Everything is just clicking, bringing a sense of harmony and peacefulness. It seems like I am starting to use parts of my brain that I have never used before. It is nice to take enjoyment in simple matters, such as putting sugar in your tea and stirring slowly.

The sun is out, the sky is blue and the ocean waves are rolling in. Sitting at the Velvet Dawn after lunch, having a beer and smoking cigarette, my over thinking mind is drawn to how we as humans describe one another. So often, we describe a person by a distinguishing feature, in order to identify the person during a conversation. We want to get to the point so quickly. Western lifestyle robs us of time to think and leaves us with not enough time for good long conversation. So we describe that person's trait as if it defines him. For example: "See, look over there, the guy with the one eyebrow."

I notice a stocky European fellow trudging up the sand toward me. He walks up to me and asks if he can join me. I say, "Sure, have a seat."

"My name is Michael. I am from England but my home is in Ireland. What about yourself?"

"My name is Brent yet recent acquaintances have called me swami. I think swami is a more fitting name while I am in India. What do you think?"

"It sounds Indian and pleasant to the ear. What brings you here?"

"The reason for traveling to India was for my best friend's wedding. After spending two weeks with his family and receiving training on being a tourist in India, it was decided that this man was ready to go it alone. I ended up in Kanyakumari or Cape Comorin for a few days and arrived here yesterday."

Mike is here with a large group of friends from London. He was here before and had a bad time but decided to give it another try. We order two beers, pour them into the large, white mugs that come with them and then hide the half-full beer bottles in the sand beside the table legs. They do not want the beer on the tables. The police may drop by and want a pay out.

Mike tells me of Indian men, snapping their own son's bones to turn them into beggars. It seems unreal. Another Indian atrocity or should I say human atrocity? You cannot blame white man or imperialism for that one, or can you?

We talk about the peddlers attempts of bullying people into making a purchase. Always doubling the store price for an item or sometimes asking more than double. Mike says to make a motion as if to strike them works well. I think that is severe and that Mike may have an attitude problem. I find saying "Poda" to be the best last resort. It is akin to saying "get lost". Ignoring a peddler and not making eye contact often results in the peddler just walking past. Do not act tough in unfamiliar surroundings.

We pour the other half of our beers into our mugs. I light a cigarette and look around. Mike is quiet for a few moments and then tells me of the people he is here with. Mike describes a second Michael, a Michael Francis that he met in a pub years ago. Catherine he describes as somewhat brain dead who is friends with Arthur. We finish our beers and Mike suggests that I meet him and his friends at the Flamingo around 5:00 p.m. for drinks and dinner. I tell him that I will be there.

I have not seen Edith today.

Walking along the beach I come up to the Flamingo. It is about 5:10 p.m. and I am taking my time because I have just had a very good joint in my room. Thank you God for the great natural marijuana. It makes the headache leave quickly. Mike and his friends are sitting around a large table that has been moved close to the ocean.

"Hello swami, let me introduce you to my friends. Please have a seat." Mike motions to the end of the table opposite of him where I take a seat. Michael is a nice guy and more cheerful than Mike. Catherine is pretty. Sandra and Neil are a couple that are on the quiet side. Arthur totally looks like a cross between Dudley Moore and Mr. Bean.

We talk about whales and fish. Mike says that he likes the snapper. I laugh and tell him that in Canada some men refer to a woman's vagina as a snapper. So Michael says, "So when you are in Canada, you should not say, 'I enjoyed the snapper here'". Too funny. Even the girls are laughing. We drink and have fun.

Mike says that the movie, *Moby Dick,* was filmed in his hometown, Yougal Co. Cork Ireland. I write a few notes during our conversation but not much of the cocktail talk. Michael asks me if I am writing a book to help my son or other father's sons. I say that it is for Keenan first and hopefully others find it entertaining and helpful in some way.

We do not order fish. Mike advises, "Never ever order fish on a Sunday here. Fishermen do not fish on Sunday. It will be fish taken in on Saturday or even Friday. They were not out with their nets last night and I did not see anyone bringing in the nets this morning."

He may be negative, but the guy seems to know what he is talking about.

Each person at the table takes turns talking a little about themselves. I mention about my father being in the hospital with cancer and that his end is near. Catherine says for me to try to have a good time but warns not too good of a time. I understand.

After being asked what I do for a living by Mike, Arthur has the balls to say, "What is brown and black and looks good on a lawyer? A Doberman!" It is funny and one of many. Of course I had to try to top him.

"So. A blond goes to see her gynecologist. She is stressed out because she thinks she is pregnant. She asks her doctor, can you get pregnant from anal sex? The doctor replies, well certainly—where do you think lawyers come from?" "That one is my favorite" I advise once the laughs and one guffaw quiets down.

Keenan, when you meet someone, keep your best news for later. Listen and do not control the conversation. Flow with it. Lead if need be. If you are not careful, you may scare your company away. Certainly, this and much of my advice may "go without saying". Nevertheless, manners are learned from people, not textbooks, Keenan.

I remain hopeful that Sonny will show up in the next few days, even though I do not think it is likely. Sonny Father does not seem to be the type of person who would enjoy the beach.

It turns out to be a very good party. Catherine and I flirt with each other subtly. At the end of the night we take the bottles and glasses up to the bar. Mike and the others leave except for Arthur, Catherine and me. Arthur is getting a little perturbed with Catherine and I whispering to each other. Catherine ignores him and we make another trip with glasses. Arthur starts to walk away. We follow behind him. Between the Velvet Dawn and their room, we stop while Arthur stops at the door of their room. It faces the Velvet Dawn.

"I will be a few minutes dear." she calls out to Arthur. He enters the room and closes the door. "You do take care of yourself swami. You are a special person. I can feel your love and energy." She takes my hand and kisses me passionately. She takes her free hand and puts it on my right shoulder. She caresses my back and then grabs my ass. I then take the liberty of softly feeling her bum. It is strong and round, just how I like them. She is not wearing panties. She kisses me well. We break off the kiss. Arthur. Too bad she is holidaying with a "friend". We say goodnight. Even though Arthur is a dork, he is human and has feelings. I would not want to get in between them if they have something going on.

It is early Monday afternoon and this newly dubbed swami feels like getting down to some serious writing. Waste no space. Cannot smoke fast enough to generate enough cigarette cardboard to write on. I prefer the cardboard over the journal because the humidity makes writing on thin paper problematic. *So here I am my son. Enjoy, you little bugger. Man I love and miss you. Sonny will show. The sun will rise for sure. This swami will receive a darker tan. He will meet more good people and have a few parties.*

I need to plan for future travel. I should stay in Kovalam for a week and then decide where to travel, after I hear more news about dad. Goa appears to be a great place to visit.

My thoughts remain turn to father dying slowly. He was hard on me, but I believe that I am a better man for it. I love him and I will miss him. *A father does not have to be hard on his son to make him good, only if he wants his son to be closer to perfection. Remember that kid.*

I think of dad, what he taught me and what you should be taught by your father. Keenan, an honest or poker face, can be both rewarding and troublesome. When a woman has spent some time with a guy with an honest face, she will quickly learn to see a lie. I am not talking about the ability to deceive. We are beyond that. The problem lies where a truthful answer will hurt her deeply. Do not lie. If she asks you something like, "Do you think that the blond over there is prettier than me?" Do not lie. If your girlfriend is a brunette and the blond is obviously better looking, reply, "Well, I am not that sure. You are certainly smarter looking and that gives bonus points. Plus you have a nicer figure." Caution, if a woman asks you such stupid bloody questions you should leave her as she is not a secure lady. You also have the option to not answer and say, "What do you think and why?"

Be happy with yourself by taking pleasure in good decision-making. Often one should first take a moment to ponder like Howard McConnell looking to the sky, in the lecture hall, when retrieving a thought. Howard was my Constitutional Law professor at the University of Saskatchewan Faculty of Law. I played chess with him on a regular basis for four years. He was my friend. I even snuck a case of beer into his office. He would smoke a cigar and I a cigarette. We had great chess matches. A game could go on for close to two hours, sometimes more. We did not skip classes to play chess. Both the Dean and Assistant Dean of Law knew what we were up to in Howard's office. We played into the evening hours many times. I spent more time playing chess in law school than studying. Did not have much time for theorists. Howard was a great thinker.

Be aware of those who look too stern or aloof. Take the time to observe. Listen. Take the time to appreciate goodness, but never condemn. That is not our place—like using the word hate. It is not healthy to hate. Be aware of the person who is too eager to do business with you. As the Dalai Lama taught, "Once bitten by a snake, even a piece of rope should seem suspicious.".

Do not concern yourself too much with details of people in your public surroundings. Messages may seem conflicting at times because I always stress awareness; not paranoia but awareness. If you are in the market for a good woman, you must be aware, strong, happy and not fat. You must have good shoulders and strong arms. You do not want skinny legs. Every young man should be working out with weights at least twice a week for one hour. From fourteen years old until you die; die old and strong. Did you know that Pierre Trudeau procreated when he was seventy-two years old!

Women can be tricky. Sometimes they may act and talk in conflict of what they want. Like the Octopussy in the Bond film 'Octopussy'. She tries to push Bond away when she actually wants him. That is not to say that 'no' does not mean 'no'. If any woman ever says no to an advance, stop. Then give her some space.

Keep in mind that your wife or girlfriend will want to talk to you; a lot. If you are not big time into listening for hours on end, especially if your occupation requires you to listen to people all day, find yourself a lady who lives to read. If you are a reader, which you are, you better not settle on a non-reader, no matter how beautiful she may be.

Be subtle when checking out a woman. Remember the two-second rule. Do not look at her for more than two seconds. Do not look at one particular body part for more than a moment (a moment is less than a second). If you look at her again make sure you smile. You know how to be happy. You are a happy guy. Show the world that you are happy. Do not turn out to be like your father and frown or scowl a lot of the time. The trouble with me is that when I think, I have a thinking face, which unfortunately looks like a frown or scowl; an intense face, for an intense thinker. In any event, as I get older and wiser I find myself smiling much more, without even trying. Especially when good women are around. If you look, her eyes catch yours and you have a serious face or scowl on, she will think you are leering. That is not good. Look her in the eyes and smile. It takes less work to smile.

Keenan, if you choose to gaze at a painting in a gallery and you enjoy it, would you not smile? If you see a beautiful woman and enjoy looking for a moment or two, smile. She will appreciate it and likely smile back.

I ought not to actively look for Catherine. Not because of bad luck or bad Karma, but because it will bring anxiety. I will talk to her again sometime. I am sure of that.

Keenan, all too often a beautiful woman will cast a spell on you. This will happen if you are mentally weak and thinking of sex too much. No doubt it may seem worth it in the short term but often a shit storm results. Strong sexual desire and a weak mind are a very bad combination, especially if someone does not love their own person and God. Whatever will be will be. You cannot make certain things happen in life but you can see foreshadowing indicators of what may occur if your mind is at rest. If you want certain wishes in your life to become reality, you have to be positive and believe that they will happen; whether meeting a nice lady or financial success. You also have to get off your ass and work hard.

Some people say you should knock off five years when guessing the age of a mature woman. Do not entertain the request of guessing a lady's age as ladies do not like to discuss their age. To me, a woman does not reach the apex of beauty until she has child or turns forty years of age. It is not just the body but the heart, soul and maturity in her thoughts. This is, of course, assuming that she is not a loon. Women are inherently evil. Be open for the exception but do not seek her. Your soul mate will come to you if you are positive about it. Be patient and be aware.

The best and worst quality in a man is the desire to be intimate with a beautiful woman. Once met, following genuine conversation and some flirtation following drinks, the woman may be on your mind for the most part of the following day. You wonder when you may see her again. Why did Catherine have to kiss me with such passion? *Women are great company. Do not ever think that women are inferior to men. The opposite is likely true. We will not get into that as this is a man's book.*

Son, never fall in love with a woman's body; that is lust. It is okay to fall in love with her heart and mind as long as her body is good from your prospective. Do not settle for second best. If she is too pretty, she is likely high maintenance. Try to meet a lady who is creative. She also must be able to golf and make salad. If she does not like to cook that is okay, just barbeque outside and have some beers.

If she does not like to clean house, that is also okay. Just make sure that you make enough money so you can hire a cleaning lady once a week. If she cannot express love, run away from her. If she is not good at making love, teach her. If she cannot be taught to be a good lover, you must leave her. That is why I prefer the older, experienced lady. When I was twenty-one years old, I had a girlfriend for a few months that was forty-two years old—it was great.

Keenan, look out for the Pat. They are those who confuse you as to whether they are Patrick or Patricia. Some Pats actually want to confuse you as to their gender. I think those people are a bit evil. Those that publicly confuse their gender are lost and that is unfortunate.

Randy Orr and I were playing Hackysack in front of his house on Saskatchewan Crescent in Saskatoon, Saskatchewan. It was Canada Day, around 11:00 a.m. back in law school. There is a Pat across the street in the park. Deep green hat pulled down, sunglasses, long sleeved sweat-shirt, dark baggy pants. This person showed no sign of gender. Lurking about, going behind bushes, coming back. Acting weird. I felt like approaching Pat, but the Hackysack was going too well.

It is a nice afternoon at the Velvet Dawn so I decide to order a beer and ice water. I feel great and remain in the mood of contemplation and writing.

The honest face is an asset in the courtroom, the bedroom, the golf course or when you threaten to kick some guy's ass. It is so simple. Do not lie. Of course you are free to slightly exaggerate a story for the sole purpose of entertaining others. Simply put, just do not deceive anyone for your own benefit nor compromise your integrity for anyone. You sell your own soul if you do that kid.

It is my second beer and it tastes better than the first. The peddlers come right up to my table and say, "Buy, buy, buy." I feel like holding up a sign that reads: "I DO NOT WANT TO BUY ANYTHING, SO BUGGER OFF PLEASE".

There is Michael. It seems that he is happy as usual, until he speaks. "How are you doing there swami?" He asks.

"Pretty damn good there Mikey boy! Top of the afternoon!"

Mike says, "You know what I saw last night swami? I saw them dig a fifteen-foot hole in the sand and bury a truckload of shit in the middle of the beach. Fancy that lad!"

Realizing that he may be on a bit of a downer since a few of his friends have left, I do not want to question him as to the relevance or meaning of his talk. But I cannot resist leading him and ask, "So, Mikey boy, you are telling me that the Indians are so hard up for a place to bury their shit that they have to dig up sand simply because it is easier to dig?"

Somewhat irritated Michael responds, "So ya don't believe me boy. Well I'll tell ya. They drain the sewage right into the ocean out there." He points to an area about eighty yards out between two popular swimming areas. "You can see bubbles rising from the ocean floor."

"I believe you Mike, about the bubbles. It just seems so stupid to dig a hole in the beach. You would think that they would have a town dump for their garbage."

"They do many things here that are stupid swami. Enough of that. Let's enjoy some beer and I will tell you about England."

"Sounds good to me big guy."

Mike carries the conversation for about an hour and he then leaves.

Later that day while swimming I would find many bubbles rising up from the ocean floor. I have decided to stay away from that part of the ocean for the rest of the stay.

Like a blackjack table Keenan, if things are not working out in plan A, go to plan B. Sometimes it is good to have four plans. Does everything happen for a reason? I doubt it. But if you rely on your instinct, walk slowly. Use the raw method. Relax and win. Focus. Do not waste valuable positive thinking time on needless worry. It is nice when your brain is sharp. Trust it all the time. I read or heard once, that if we knew how powerful our brains were we would not have a negative thought again. The point is easily understood but cannot be taken literally. There is a little more to it, yet it can be learned.

There is a familiar voice. "Hello swami, have you had lunch yet?" I turn to the left and Edith is standing below me.

"No, I have not. It is nice to see you Edith. What do you have in mind dear?" I ask.

"I am meeting someone at the Jungle Restaurant in a few minutes. I think that you and he will really hit it off well."

"Thank you for the invitation. Sounds good to me." The sun highlights Edith's warm eyes and her pretty face.

We enter the Lonely Planet or what some call the Jungle Restaurant, which is really cool. Guess some call it the latter is because it is in the middle of a small jungle. We follow a narrow sandy path, zig-zagging through the trees to get here. There is an European looking guy about my age sitting at a table that Edith approaches. Edith's friend is about thirty-one years old. His hair is short, light brown and has a neat wave to it. His hair has partially receded yet not enough to make him look like a dork. He is of medium build and is somewhat lanky, but not skinny. He dresses like a hippy but not all-out hippy wearing a bandanna like Aunt Jemima or anything. He is wearing shorts and a tee-shirt. What is on the tee-shirt shows a laid back attitude; lines of colored zebras running up into the sky at a forty-five degree angle.

Edith introduces us. "Gunvald, this is swami and swami, this is Gunvald."

Gunvald stands up, shakes my hand, looks me in the eyes and says, "I am pleased to meet you swami."

I say, "Likewise Gunvald, it is my pleasure."

Gunvald has seen a whale twice the length of an oil barge. He says that he has grown up as a whaleman. He is from Oslo, Norway. His grandfather was a whaler from Western Norway.

Sitting down at the table for four, in his Norwegian accent that has a neat nasal drawl to it, he states, "My maternal Uncle was a whaler. My grandfather was harpooner." Gunvald tells us how he climbed the mast of a whaling ship. He is clearly into telling me about whaling because he is an observant fellow. He sees that I am holding *Moby Dick* in my left hand. He also recognizes that I am most interested in what he has to say. This swami has just met a lifelong friend.

Gunvald describes a more modern form of whale hunting than that told by Melville. Gunvald describes the modern, post-industrial type of whale hunting where harpoon guns are used and not harpoon throwing. I guess guys like the tattooed Queequeg are out of work.

Gunvald and Edith are seeing a friend off this afternoon. I decide to give them privacy and tell them that I would see them later and that I would be at my usual afternoon hangout, the Velvet Dawn, after swimming.

A few hours later I see Gunvald walking up the beach. "Hello swami." Gunvald calls out and waves. He walks up the steps and sits across from me at my usual table.

Gunvald relates, "If you are not radical when you are young you will not have a heart. If you are not conservative when you are old, you have no brain."

"Yes Gunvald. Our sociology professor reminded the class once that we may be lefty New Democrats now, but that will change once we leave the university and start to make good money."

"That is right swami."

"Swami, I am a socialist for now. I hope to be one for a long time."

"Wait until you get married and your lady likes to fine dine." I reply.

"What is wrong with eating a good meal?"

"Nothing so long as it is not in some hoity-toity place with hoity-toity people. I cannot put on airs. I do not like fake people, whether it is a fake attitude or a fake plastic face." I vent.

We talk of music and literature. He does not think I talk too much. He talks just as much. It's all good.

"How did you injure your toe Gunvald?"

"New Years. I fell down the stairs leading to my room."

Gunvald and I have another round. We talk politics, the world economy and our studies. We get along very well.

It is just before sunset and Edith joins us with her friend Tanya. Gunvald and Tanya have met before. Harry appears out of nowhere and joins us. "Hey swami. Hello Gunvald." Harry happily announces. We shake hands. I have gotten to know the bookish looking waiter here named Muriel. I call out to him. "Muriel, please bring us more beer."

Edith says, "Thank you for ordering swami."

"You are welcome Edith. Harry, did you have a busy day at work?" I ask.

Harry replies, "It was not bad. Steady enough not to get bored." We finish our beers and walk over to Santana's to eat. We go to My Dream after eating and the five of us close the place with laughter.

I decide to forgo the Velvet Dawn for breakfast and try My Dream for coffee and toast. My Dream is a small coffee house during the day. It has a covered interior with an open beach patio. It is the only place that stays open past midnight. The manager has to pay off the police for serving liquor after hours and during hours for that matter. The police have a guy that comes by on a busy night to keep track of how much alcohol is sold.

The bathroom at My Dream is not that great. You have to navigate through a narrow hallway past the kitchen. Once inside you must use caution in the small and dimly lit room. The hole is small so you squat to pee and aim well. It is much easier to walk over to the ocean to urinate. Other than the bathroom, My Dream is fabulous. Edith totally likes My Dream.

She says it is her dream bar. The outdoor beach patio has eight tables that can seat six to eight people each. The view of the bay is fantastic from here and we are close to the point. You can see the lighthouse at the other end of the bay and much of the massive beach. When the tide is out the beach is extremely wide to the ocean. The coffee is hot and strong. The jam on my toast is sweet.

Man has a good number of weaknesses. Put a non-drinker in the right (or wrong) place and time and he may become an alcoholic. The Swedish alcoholic is seen drunk often. He walks by and all of the workers in the Santana bar leer intensely. Waiting. Waiting for the drunk bugger to insult them by yelling out as he did before, "You are selling you poison. It is all poison!"

It is morning, you silly Swede, I think. He looks like he has been drinking for more than twenty-four hours. For three years straight I am told that he has been here—drunk most of the time. He does it again when he passes Santana's and walks in front of My Dream. "You are all drinking poison!" he screams. He looks like he just woke up drunk from a few hours earlier or if he did not take a break at all. He staggers. Yep, he's pissed drunk. Before 11:00 a.m.. The sleepy staff ignore him this time. He was drunk two days earlier in the early afternoon at the Velvet Dawn. I return to my room.

Gunvald must be sleeping. I will go to the ocean a little later and wake up some more. New neighbors have arrived on both sides of my room, two ladies and a man from Denmark. They advise that they are on a spiritual pilgrimage and they are taking a little holiday at Kovalam for a few days. Their respective travels led them to the North and now to the South. I hear the girls giggling after I blow pot smoke over the wall of my bathroom. There is a one-foot gap between the concrete walls and the concrete ceiling. I wash some clothes, do a count of my Rupees and tidy up the room.

While sitting at my usual chair at Velvet Dawn, I realize that it is nice to be a creature of habit. There is less decision making and you spend much less time looking for your stuff if you habitually put your stuff where it belongs, not like in the black hole of a purse. Muriel brings me a beer without me asking. He knows it is afternoon and it is beer time.

I walk over to Muriel to tell him that I was going to my room for ten minutes and ask him to watch my table. I turn and step. Suddenly I am falling. Left foot caught the edge of the wall and ten feet below is the ground. Left hand bracing the fall. Plump! No rocks, the sand is soft and much better than what you see in many golf course bunkers. My left shoulder is buggered up while my left elbow somewhat strained. I look up at Muriel smiling with embarrassment. He grins back.

"Are you okay, swami buddy?"

"Yes, if one falls it is best to fall on a beach."

I get up and limp to my room. I know of three different remedies for the pain.

Washing out the scrape on my arm, I think that it would be cool to swim in all of the world's oceans and see all the wonders this great world has to offer.

I smoke a third of a reefer and the pain ebbs quickly. I am walking carefully. Funny thing is, accidents like a fall usually occur late, after a night of drinking, not during a sober, early afternoon.

The beer that I left is no longer cold. I catch Muriel's eye.

"Can you bring another one please Muriel?"

"Yes, swami Sir. Let's put the cap back on this one and put it in the secret cooler."

"Thank you Muriel my man."

Looking out on the beach I see some tourists basking in the sun. Three pale British women and a swarthy muscular guy are lying on beach towels. He is looking at two young Indian men in black pants and white collared shirts. They are staring at one of his lady friend's crotch, or outline thereof on her bikini bottoms.

He is muscular, has a good skin tone and looks tough. He gets up and looks at the Indian men straight in the eyes. He says to them, "You are dirty. You are dirty little men for eyeing up the ladies bodies and joking about it amongst yourselves." He goes on to say that if they were in London he would be knocking heads. I could not agree more.

I write for an hour, until beads of sweat drip on my journal. It is time for some exercise in my favorite form, a big swim. The waves are small, however, the swimming is good. I swim out a far way and feel safe about it. It is good not to think of sharks for two reasons. First, it is unlikely that sharks are close by as the coast deepens gradually here with the waves rolling for a long time. Sharks do not like to body surf. Secondly, worrying is a total waste of good energy. Walking out of the water onto the beach feeling quite salty, I think that maybe it is time to get the salt off before returning to the Velvet Dawn. The dried salt on your bathing suit and body itches you in the heat.

> Salt on shorts. Sand on floor.
> So much ocean salt.
> Water purifies.
> We are water.
> Water cleanses
> Your clothes,
> Your body,
> So good.
> Creator love us.
> Thank you world and water.

Gunvald arrives and takes a seat beside me. We look at the women on the beach. Overpopulation, according to Gunvald, is often misused as a reason for poverty or corruption. He concludes that a weak national government, grossly slow bureaucracy and religious based political parties are major factors that hold India back. The world lacks a good model of a democracy that actually works for the benefit of most. I understand what he is getting at.

I say, "Gunvald, history has shown that wealthy nations survive on the backs of poorer nations, just as wealthy people survive by keeping the poor masses down. The world is being threatened by a cultural seduction for wealth and fame. If people could only love others more and not dwell on their respective egos. Times are changing quickly. Globalization is helping India's economy to begin roaring like a lion. Colonialism is dead."

We soon end conversing over the subject as we both agree and acknowledge the basic issues facing poor countries and poor people in wealthy countries—capitalism with greed.

Gunvald says, "When I was in South Africa, spending time drinking with my best friend from Yugoslavia, he was taught to make cheers in the Norwegian fashion, you hold your beer up and then grab your friends balls."

"What? That is a dangerous way of doing cheers." I exclaim.

"It is only done with certain friends. It is not a cross-cultural thing swami."

"Well no doubt Gunvald." I point out. "That move could result in the grabber getting pummeled, especially if the victim has his nards squeezed too hard. Are you shitting me Gunvald?" "Shitting you?" He asks. He reads my look of contempt and says, "Oh, am I bull shitting you? Yes. However there is a little truth to the story."

We decide to rent some boogie boards when we see Edith and her lady friend, Nancy, walking up the beach toward us. Gunvald says to me, "Let's ask Edith and Nancy if they want to join us in riding boogie boards."

"Good idea Gunvald. The more the merrier."

"Hello Edith." Gunvald says. "Hello Nancy. Have you met swami, Nancy?"

"Briefly the other day." Nancy replies. "Hello swami."

"Hello Nancy. Good day Edith my dear." I say.

Gunvald inquires, "We are going to rent boogie boards. The waves are just right. Would you ladies like to join us?"

"Yes Gunvald. Let's go get them. Do you know how to boogie board swami? I bet you are good at it." Edith states.

"I am learning Edith."

The boards are ten dollars for an hour, which is a little steep. You can buy the damn things for fifty bucks back home. Next time one comes to India they should bring a couple and sell them to the board vendors upon leaving.

The boogie boards work well. You can ride the wave all the way in. It is like body surfing where you must paddle your arms and flutter your legs like heck to catch the wave. The four of us have a great time and Gunvald is marveled when Edith's nice, ample, boob slips out of her top after a tumble. She smiles and puts it back in. She is so cute with her demeanor.

It is around nine in the evening and Gunvald and I are at My Dream. We meet the Finnish girls and Gunvald invites them over to our table. Their names are Minna and Katarina. They are gorgeous women. Minna has light brown hair, just off her neck, that curls under. She is of average height. She is wearing a colorful throw. Katarina is thinner than Minna with long, straight, blond hair. She is also wearing a colorful throw. At the outset, it becomes clear that Minna likes to drink more than Katarina. Minna is a nurse while Katarina works in marketing. With a beautiful accent Minna states, "Do you have more to smoke swami?"

"Yes Minna."

"Good, good." Minna replies.

Katarina does not smoke pot and has just a good as time as the rest of us. We are talking up a storm, communication setbacks aside. Gunvald mentions that in Norway, young girls, twelve to thirteen years old, soak their tampons in spirits. What the hell is Gunvald saying? Perhaps an error on my part. How the hell did this conversation come up? We laugh. Gunvald leads the conversation and I try to listen. The more the Finnish girls drink the more high-pitched their voices become.

"You must hear this joke ladies." I state. "A fifty year old Italian man named Guido is relaxing at his favorite bar in Rome where he meets a gorgeous blonde woman. After some talk, they go back to his apartment for a drink and more talk. He makes love to her with vigor. After a moment he asks her with a smile, 'So, you finish?' She pauses for a second, frowns and replies, 'No.' Guido is surprised and reaches for her again and gives her the sausage wildly as she screams passionately."

Minna interrupts, "What is sausage swami?" I stand up and point to my crotch. "Oh, I see."

"The sex ends and again Guido asks her with a smile, 'You finish?'
Again, after a short pause, she returns his smile, cuddles him and softly
says, 'No'. Guido is stunned. He is not going to let this woman go unsatis-
fied so he reaches for her again. With the last of his strength he pleases her
again and she rips his back with her nails. Guido falls to the bed onto his
back, gasping for air. He says, 'You must be finish.' She whispers, 'No, I
am Norwegian'." The girls get it and laugh while Gunvald snorts and guffaws.

It is just past midnight. My Dream is rocking with a couple dozen revelers. Bernie joins us. He is a 'Heinz fifty-seven', but mainly of Irish and
British blood. He has long, dark, wavy hair past the base of his neck and a
trimmed beard. He is a pleasant looking fellow with a jolly smile and
demeanor. He resembles the prophet Jesus. He is not skinny like a stick
bug but does not have much fat. He is a very funny man and plays a good
guitar. His hotel is three kilometers away and he has been in India for two
weeks. He writes his name and numbers in my journal. He has wit and a
good laugh. We have one hell of a party. We meet two other men from
England, Paul and Charlie. Paul is a nice quiet man while Charlie is an
arrogant tough guy.

Gunvald and I walk back to our rooms along the beach. All of a sudden
I go down. My left foot catches a large rock. Landing face down I manage
to get both palms down to the sand to land in the push up position. My
face slaps the sand with eyes and mouth closed, despite the intoxication.

Gunvald says, "Are you okay swami?" He extends his hand and pulls
me up. One sandal is off my foot next to rock.

"*THANK YOU MAN. LOOK AT SANDAL. BIG ROCK BROKE SAN-
DAL GUNVALD. I NO WORRY. SANDAL PROBLEM WILL LOOK
AFTER ITSELF NEXT DAY.*"

"Okay swami. Why worry about a sandal anyway. At least your head
did not land on the rock."

It is morning. I am the only customer at the Velvet Dawn. Before
ordering I feel a tap on the back of my shoulder from behind. A voice says,
"You need sandal fixing Sir?"

Wow! I turn around and see a young man about twenty-seven years old with a kit in his left hand. Without getting out of my chair, I hand him my broken sandal. The young man sits down on the sand next to my table and proceeds to sew up the sandal. Just like that. I have not seen him on the beach before. He charges me one American dollar and I give him three; another wonderful result of magical India and a positive attitude.

Gunvald arrives and we order breakfast. We are having tea and toast and Gunvald looks like he could be ready for a good party tonight, if he takes care during the day. A young skinny girl, about twenty-three years old, sits on the beach in a zazen position. Gunvald notices what I am gazing at.

I ask him, "Do you think she has found herself or do you think she is still on her way?"

Gunvald answers, "Finding yourself is a selfish endeavor. Meditation can be seen as a form of copping out of the struggles that life presents."

I add in, "I think yoga is crap for me as I prefer the punching bag or gym. It is good for some women to keep their bodies in shape. Yoga and meditation helps certain people who cannot focus. You know, the types that cannot help but think or worry about two or more dilemmas at once. The problem is, they do not realize they do not have a real dilemma at all. They are worry warts. Cripes, right now, right here, if I did not have this little beer gut, I would show that young girl how to levitate!"

Gunvald laughs with a few guffaws.

Gunvald enjoys the talk and is in the mood for a swell story. It is time to tell him the testicle story. "Gunvald, I have a funny story to tell you, but before I get into the funny story from law school, I must tell you what happened about forty minutes ago. Remember last night when I tripped on the rock?"

"Yes, you fell on your face and you broke your sandal." Gunvald answers.

"Yes. Do you remember me saying that the broken sandal would look after itself next day?"

"Yes, I do."

I go on, "So I sit down here this morning and within a few minutes, a young man taps me on the shoulder and asks me, 'Do you need sandal fixing Sir?'"

"No way!" Gunval pipes.

"Yes. He fixes my sandal perfect for a buck."

"Unbelievable. You are a swami."

"I am learning."

"So what about the funny law school story?" Gunvald asks.

"It is called the testicle story. A few years before law school I had this girlfriend. We met while we were in nursing college. She was quite skinny. Without getting into crude details I will simply say that my left testicle got injured while we were exercising. As time passed by my left testicle grew larger and larger. I noticed it, of course, but wrote it off thinking it was a result of a childhood injury when I was three years old, fell off my bike and smashed my little nuts against the crossbar of the bike. Because I was sexually active I thought that the left one was working overtime and the right one not at all."

"Snort, hee, hee." Gunvald is having trouble holding it in.

"Let me finish before you piss yourself, okay?"

"Okay swami. You are crazy."

"I know. So by first year law school, the left testicle has grown to the size of a tennis ball."

Gunvald interjects, "A tennis ball?"

"Yes. A freaking tennis ball. I showed it to my law school buddy, Garth, during a first year post-exam party and before you know it he had me pulling the bloody thing out at parties and displaying it to women for laughs."

"Did it get you laid?" Gunvald asks.

"Of course not. Most women were too shocked to be interested. Plus, I would simply hold the testicle in my left hand, while keeping my sausage in my boxer shorts with my right hand. Good question though."

"Okay, go on."

"I went tree planting in British Columbia that summer and returned home in August. I stood on my grandmother's deck at her cabin in

Crooked Lake, Saskatchewan. My mother and grandmother were sitting on a couch in the veranda

Gunvald says, "No, you did not pull that thing out and show your grandmother."

I answer, "Well, I sure as hell did. So I pull it out and like usual, let it lay on the palm of my left hand. By this time it is a little larger than a tennis ball."

"So I agree with the hospital thing and ask her not to get too excited and tell her it does not hurt. My mother said, 'I do not care if it hurts or not. Something is not right with that nut.'"

Gunvald is now bent over in his chair laughing, salivating and almost hyperventilating. I am also having trouble keeping my composure.

Laughingly, I say to my buddy, "Gunvald, my mother took me to the hospital in Melville first thing in the morning. Dr. Frangou immediately sends us to Regina, Saskatchewan to see a specialist. Once I saw the specialist he booked me for surgery the next day."

Gunvald has almost had enough because he is laughing so hard, snot is running down his nose and tears streaming down his cheeks. He says to me, "You are killing me swami. What the hell was wrong with your nut?"

"There is a sheath around your testicles. It produces a fluid that surrounds your testicle and protects it. The specialist said that I must have injured the sheath. He said that I must have been kicked in the nuts or that the poor bugger was subject to being bounced against a hard surface."

Gunvald has calmed down a bit now but he still looks at me like I am crazy.

"The specialist urologist asked me about my sex life. I told him about the skinny girl. As professional as he tried to be, he still could not stop the smirk on his face from forming. The next day, I got surgery and the surgeon removed the sheath around my left testicle. I woke up in mild pain."

"I guess swami. I hope they gave you good drugs."

"A little morphine. However, it turned out that the charge nurse had a twisted sense of humor. She sent in the sexiest, youngest, nurse in the surgical unit to come and do post-op peri-care."

Gunvald asks, "What do you mean?"

"Post-op means post operation. After surgery, the incision on my scrotum needed to be cleaned. The sexy young nurse that came in to check and clean had long black hair past her shoulders in a ponytail."

"I like a long black ponytail on a woman. They are so feminine and sexy." Gunvald adds.

"Toot shooting they are Gunvald. The nurse introduced herself as Sally. She was wearing a light blue nursing uniform that was a dress, just down to her knees, with a zipper from top to bottom. She had a large bosom. Her face was very pretty. Her zipper was lowered just enough to reveal a few inches of cleavage. A good hint of sexiness."

"I hope you are going to end this part of the story soon. I am getting excited."

"Okay Gunvald. So she started to wash my scrotum softly and I began to get erect. I did not want an erection. I have six sutures and …"

Gunvald stops me by saying, "Okay swami, I know that you are a poet and could go on forever. Obviously you cannot have the nurse. What next?"

"Well my friend, I end up in Saskatoon a few days later in order to register for second year of law school. After completing the paperwork, the students end up at the Labatt's Brewery for a back to school party.

Gunvald nods and says, "Cool. Out of the hospital and into a brewery."

"So I was talking to two classmates from first year law about their respective summers. I should tell you now that the only way I could walk or move was to take six ice cubes and put them in a baggy. You know, a sandwich bag and double bag it. I had to get some jockey shorts as boxers were out of the question and so was tape. So there I was with a Kotex like pad full of ice cooling the pain in my nards talking to the ladies."

"Okay, I think I see the ending now." Gunvald predicts.

"Yes, the sandwich bags broke their seals and water started to drip down my left leg. One of the girls saw this and asked me, 'Brent, what are you doing? Are you peeing yourself?' I said 'No way'. I turned around, took the sandwich bags from my crotch and threw them and the rest of the ice in a trash barrel a few feet away. The girls were teeming with inquisitiveness. I turn to them and was compelled to tell them the testicle story."

Gunvald exclaims, "That is one hell of a round story. I wish I could have seen the expression on the ladies faces." We laugh hard. Muriel comes over to find out what he is missing.

We are at My Dream. Gunvald, Minna, Katarina, Paul and I sit together. Charlie and some others are a table away. I ask Charlie, "Have you ever surfed in other countries beside Britain and India?" He mumbles, "arghhh, duh, I dunno … burp … maybe Vietnam." I ask because I want to find out if his inner character has some good within his egotistical shell.

I ask the same question, "Have you surfed in other countries besides Britain, India or Vietnam?" The response again is gargled and slurred. None of us can understand what he is saying. After he realizes that he is not being funny, he says in a more controlled voice, "Oh, I thought you asked me if I ever served in Vietnam!" What a complete jerk!

For some reason, after a couple of hours of drinking, we decide to go to Charlie's room after a few drinks. He lures Minna and our group there by saying that he has extra special smoke at his flat. He has the hots for Minna. We share a smoke. Then Charlie starts to act like a crazed cave-man. Right in front of us, he says something unintelligible and slaps Minna on the side of her face. Not hard, but forceful enough to be heard and to move her head. Gunvald and I look at each other with eyebrows and tempers raised. What the hell was that? Bernie also looks dumb-founded.

I say, "Friends, let us go for a walk. Charlie is obviously drunk and see-ing demons. No offence Charlie, but what you did just now is not accept-able behavior no matter the circumstances. You never, ever, hit a woman, no matter what. Even if she shuts you down and uses an insult." He looks down and does not make a sound.

We leave and walk on the beach towards the ocean. We stop by an abandoned boat in front of My Dream. I say to Bernie, "I know that Minna is not my sister but you must keep Charlie away from her. I do not know why you even talk to that asshole. He hit her. Please take care of her."

"Okay, I will swami." Bernie answers.

I leave with Gunvald after deciding to shut things down and catch up on some sleep.

Walking down the beach under the morning sun, I finally give in and buy a drum from the young boy drum peddler, who has asked me to buy every day. It is for Keenan. The waves are big today. I will go out and get hit big. I take the drum to the room and get ready for a swim.

Gunvald arrives at the Velvet Dawn. We shake hands and knock foreheads. You can tell that he is upset with Charlie because he shakes his head and says, "Great time last night but that Brit." He goes on, "The character of Charlie is a good example of how not to act. He acts arrogant. Too many men because of their muscles, premature baldness turned into a shaved head, along with some booze to give them extra strength, brings such a false sense of superiority."

"Gunvald, I could not agree more. The young people today prancing around listening to rap music, thinking they are cool because they have a gold necklace, the crotch of their pants at their knees, a crooked hat and have rhythm. A bad attitude is not good and only leads to trouble."

Gunvald says, "Charlie is an abuser."

"Charlie slapped Minna in the face. He had no reason to. He must be banned from our group—not that he was ever part of it anyways. A good man never hits a female."

"We should teach Charlie a lesson and kick the shit out of him." Gunvald states. "Let's do it only if he provokes us one more time."

"Agreed Gunvald. I can see the comeuppance of Charlie clearly."

We are both somewhat hung over. Gunvald is more so as my swim in the ocean helped clear my head and blood earlier. In his usual baritone nasal Norwegian accented voice, Gunvald says, "Do you want to have some big waves. They look good. Listen to them."

"I was thinking of getting hit big. Get some exercise and survive some fear."

"Let's go out and see if we can body surf."

"Yes Gunvald. I want the waves to rock me and beat the rest of the pleasant hangover out." The waves are big, loud and boisterous; almost threatening. Come on swami, they are threatening. Piss off alter ego. This sober swami sees the waves as friends. We ride a few in and take a breather close to shore and talk about last night some more.

Gunvald is of the opinion that we ought to have done a little more regarding Minna's safety and bodily sanctity around Charlie. He surmises, "I am sure that Charlie has some positive qualities. On occasion, we sometimes find ourselves steering the conversation or our group, but what Charlie did last night was not just negative, it was reprehensible. It almost seemed that he was trying to get laid and impress Minna by acting like a tough asshole, while treating her like shit all at the same time. No conscience, little self awareness and very little feeling for others."

"Sounds like a touch of evilness to me brother." I say. "We could not have prevented the slap Gunvald. Let's leave it at that. Charlie is a piece of camel dung. Bernie knows it. He will no longer sit beside Charlie, not only because of the slap but also because he is taken with Minna. We should not waste energy on Charlie. Furthermore, I believe that he will cower and keep his distance from our table in the future."

Gunvald and I wade out into the ocean. We stop when we can no longer touch bottom and tread water. Big waves are coming in. They usually come in sets of three or fives here, sometimes as many as seven consecutive waves will tumble in. The key is to miss the first one or two and focus on the larger third.

In order to let a wave pass without crushing your bones, you must dive into the heart of the oncoming wave and spring yourself up and through the wave like a dolphin. The wave should pass by overhead and spurt you out toward the sky. You need to arch your back through the entire maneuver. Sometimes spurting out of a wave is as much fun as catching a good ride.

Catching a wave is not rocket science. You just have to swim like heck toward the shore so that by the time the wave reaches you, it is below your waist and you can stiffen up and ride the baby. You also must have your arms straight out at a forty-degree angle from your head and your palms facing down. You also have to have your legs flexed and again your back arched. If you do all this and if you are fortunate to be swimming fast enough when the wave arrives you will catch a good ride.

Five big ones are coming fast. I dive through the first two. The space between the crests is good. I reverse myself and start swimming hard to shore. It is going to happen. Suddenly, I am at the wave's crest and moving fast with the wave. I can feel the rushing water moving fast, with bubbles and foam tickling my chest and stomach. Water squirts through my armpits. The wave carries me swiftly. Butterflies develop; the good kind, the kind that made a seven year old me go "Weeeeee" when dad drove up and down through the Qu'Appelle Valley hilly roads at eighty miles per hour. The wave takes me all the way to shore. I jump up and make a thumbs up and beam at the sky. Man I love being alive! There are so many natural beauties on earth.

We catch many good waves in the next hour. Gunvald and I are almost oblivious to each other. Looking over and checking once in a while, making our respective moves with the waves. We both know that the waves are at their best just now and talking will take away from our surfing with them.

"Let's take a break and have a drink at the Velvet Dawn swami." Gunvald suggests.

"Good idea, buddy."

My hair is bad today. The humidity makes it lay down flat resulting in a roman look. It is too long. So I ask him, "Gunvald, what do you think about my hair?"

"You look like a dork!" he answers.

"Why so?"

"Because you look like a dork. Have you been in India so long that you forget what a dork looks like?" he says with a wide grin. I laugh. He is fooling and playing on a silly weakness. I would rather be a cue ball than have flat dork hair. I ask Muriel for a beer and Gunvald orders a Pepsi.

I think, Pepsi, who is the dork you Slavic icicle? And say, "Well I may be a dork for having a bad hair afternoon, you are a dork for being a stick!"

Certainly, it is okay to drink Pepsi, but if you plan or honestly expect to get tight in the evening, start earlier so you can enjoy the morning the next day. It is better to start at four in the afternoon and end your party within hours of midnight. It is not good to sleep past 10:00 a.m., especially when you are at the beach. It is bad luck to sleep past noon and the best time to be on the beach is between 10:00 a.m. and 2:00 p.m..

We decide to go for lunch at the Lonely Planet. Gunvald eats vigorously. Gunvald's Thali meal appears to enthrall him as he has many different sauces on the sides of the round tin plate. This place is Gunvald's favorite place to eat lunch. I eat my chicken curry. There is not much talking. The way it should be when men eat.

Moving from the Jungle, we head to our mid-afternoon drinking spot at the Velvet Dawn. As we walk the subject of women comes up again. Gunvald has Minna on the brain and I have life. The air is so fresh. The brain is so fresh. Swimming and body surfing for three hours clears the mind and body of last night's cobwebs. The insight and mellow understanding of so much is electrifying yet humbling. The energy of the universe is felt. The beauty of the forces required to make the earth spin, the sunshine and the waves roll in just right so we can ride them is appreciated. Nothing troubles me. I enjoy walking along this path meandering under the ceiling of the palm trees.

Keenan, do not be too hyper and exercise. Big shoulders need exercise; otherwise your neck will suffer. Learn to relax. Find your inner peace on your own as religion will only get in the way. Take time to eat. Take time to work. Take time to sleep. Take time to help others. Take time to drink when you are old enough. Take time to be with friends. Take time to golf. Try not to get caught up in the turmoil of Western life.

Gunvald and I sit down at our usual table. Muriel brings us beer. I say to Gunvald, "The waves were so good before lunch. We both caught some good ones."

"Let's only have two beers each before we go in."

"Sounds good to me Gunvald."

The ocean is cool at first. Warmth surrounds me, I get up to my chest and dive under. The salt on my lips is friendly. Quietly standing in the ocean, I look up to the sun, with my eyes squinting, feeling the warmth of her rays. A sense of belonging to the world and the grand scheme of things hit me. The ocean does this to you.

My thoughts are interrupted by Gunvald when he states, "If you take a few shots from Charlie, you may get lucky with Katarina."

"It is not hard to almost hate that arrogant, dumb ass bastard even though it is not good to hate." I reply.

While treading water and waiting for the waves, we decide that if Charlie angers us again, harsh measures will result. Gunvald exclaims, "We are going to treat him like he were a Nazi in Norway. We will fuck him up with no sympathy at all."

"Cool heads must prevail my friend. If the situation arises, after giving him the chance to leave the bar and be banished from our group, that we have to beat him, we must make sure that we are correct and that we have outside support. If we shut Charlie down, we need to be able to deal with the authorities. Besides Gunvald, as I said before, Charlie will hang his head like a convicted pedophile and keep his distance from us."

An hour passes by, with the waves carrying us well. Holy Lick! Gunvald just missed springing through a huge wave. The wave is tossing him around like a tumbleweed blown by a strong dry prairie wind. His limbs resemble daddy long legs scrambling along the ocean floor. Bending, twisting with so much give. Oh, that must hurt. I begin to worry. I hope he comes up. There he is. Now I can laugh, and do I.

"Gunvald you bugger! Are you all right?"

He does not respond at first. He shakes his head, trying to get the sand out of his left ear. He says with his usual grunt, "Argghhhh, swami, that was wild. I did not think I was going to come up!"

I respond, "Well you sand-farting, flexible fucker, you certainly deserve a few beers."

So off we go.

We get henna paintings after some beers and ice water, then go to my room, which should be called the 'swami smoking shack', and smoke one and a half. Both of us, smiley faced, are feeling no pain whatsoever.

We practice the head wiggle. Gunvald is laughing and snorking; the all too funny nasal voice laugh where he emits a guffaw, snort or snork. The head wiggle is difficult as we are accustomed to shaking our head side to side for 'no' and nodding for 'yes'.

Gunvald and I return to the Velvet Dawn for a beer. Ten minutes later Bernie arrives. Bernie says that the British are no 'cup of tea'. He has fine ambitions and intentions. He came to India to sit on the beach and relax. We talk of cricket and football. It is nice to spend time with him, during a partially sober afternoon, when we are not drinking late at My Dream. It is a good change.

While Bernie sleeps on the beach, his room is just around the bend. He says that he has not slept in his bed yet and has slept on the beach for almost two weeks. It seems that it is either too late for Bernie or that he is too drunk to make it home half the time. No wonder. He is staying, or not staying, at a hostel for three hundred Rupees for two weeks. The sand is probably more comfortable.

Bernie has superior guitar playing skills as opposed to Charlie. It is nice to listen to him play so long as he does not sing. Bernie is funny as hell. His humor is very much the Monty Python, Northern British or Carry on Camping type humor with a twist. The twist happens to be that it is more than just stand up comedy, it is well placed, witty and intelligent humor. He does not look like anyone famous yet he is distinguished looking. Do not get me wrong. Bernie is a good-looking guy—masculine yet caring. He is a gentleman and a good party companion.

We talk about how small the world can be. The time passes so quickly when you are having so much enjoyment socializing with people from different far away lands. *Keenan, for your nineteenth birthday I am definitely bringing you here. Kanyakumari, Dehli, the Taj Mahal, Bombay and Goa are on the list.*

The funniest thing is heard from a short distance down the beach. "Some grasses, sunglasses, some grasses."

"What the hell is that Bernie?" I ask.

Without turning around Bernie says, "It is the sunglass man swami."

Gunvald and I turn to our left and see and hear him say, "Sunglasses, some grasses, sunglasses."

The sunglass man is tall, skinny and comical. He wears a long jacket that has more than a hundred pairs of sunglasses pinned to the inside and outside. He is always smiling ear to ear when you see him. He is known as the sunglass man. There are even postcards with his caricature on them. When he calls out, advertising his sunglasses, everyone is sure that he is also saying, 'some grasses'.

Bernie advises that the Sunglass Man only sells sunglasses and does very well at that.

Sunglass Man waves at Bernie and walks over to our table. His voice is so cool. It is high-pitched and quite rhythmical. "How are you boys doing this afternoon? Beer tasting good Bernie lad?"

"It is refreshing." Bernie answers and introduces us. We do not feel bad about not buying any sunglasses as Bernie bought five pairs earlier on separate occasions. We share a beer and a cigarette with him. The sunglass man is definitely one of the coolest guys on the beach. One could say that he has the best job on the planet, if not for the monsoon season.

Sunglass man finishes his beer and cigarette and as he leaves he says, "Thank you for the cigarette and glass of beer boys. Back to business now."

He walks away and the sound of "Some grasses, sunglasses, some grasses ..." is heard less and less as he walks down the beach.

I suggest, "Bernie, let's all of us get together for dinner tonight. I see the Finnish girls on the beach by Santana's. Why don't you go suggest dinner and ask the ladies to pick a spot. Gunvald can go with you and say hello while I ensure that his beer does not get warm."

"Good idea swami." Gunvald says.

"I agree swami." Bernie adds. "I will see you tonight."

"Later Bernie."

Gunvald returns and says, "They want to eat next door, right after sunset."

"That is good Gunvald. We should let Edith and Harry know. I am sure that Bernie will run into Paul."

Gunvald looks for his beer. "Where is my beer swami?"

"I said that I would not let it become warm so I had to drink it. Muriel is on his way now, only steps behind you." Muriel puts two beer on the table.

"Thanks buddy."

"You are most welcome Gunvald. After we finish up here and have our respective showers meet me at my room for a smoke."

Gunvald replies, "Good idea swami. I am not big on long showers so I won't be that long."

I say, "You can't have long showers here because the water is cool."

Gunvald finishes by saying, "Instant shrinkage."

Gunvald and I arrive at the restaurant and see that Minna and Katarina are already seated at a long table with some guy who looks like a fancy boy. He is introduced as Andy. I will call him Dandy Andy.

Andy met Minna during the afternoon. It is quite evident he is trying to impress her. He is fancy boy with fancy hair and a fake fancy smile. He talks of Green Peace and is proudly wearing a Green Peace shirt. He mainly talks to Minna and does not let anyone else join in on the conversation. Bernie shows up and Andy does not talk to Bernie either. Dandy Andy is the poster boy for those with the usual 'I am holier than thou' attitude. He will not last long with our group as no one holds court around us or within us.

Edith and Harry arrive. At least there is some good joking going around the table now aside from the serious talk from Dandy Andy to Minna. You can tell that Bernie does not like Dandy Andy's company either. I interrupt Dandy holding court and ask the table, "Should I get us a box of beer from next door? The waiter tells me he is out." Andy looks away perturbed.

My friends agree with nods and squeaky Finnish affirmations, except for Dandy Andy. He stays quiet for a two second pause and then rudely says, "Again, now where was I?" I think, fuck you Andy, you ass, someone must get us beer. He angers me, which is difficult to do after smoking some pot earlier. Nevertheless, I imagine punching him so hard that he will fly out of his chair. I despise those who go on and on about how great they are, trying to impress others. Some people are simply socially retarded and it is best just to let it go. *Keenan your old man may drink a little too much for some people's liking but at least he is not a pompous ass. Can I say this; to be a good person you must be aware of your actions while ensuring that you do good and cause no harm or discomfort to anyone.*

Bernie, the witty shit, calls out, "Andy, for the millionth time, don't bloody exaggerate!" Then he says, "I do not like people who generalize, they are all the same." He is with me. Andy does not acknowledge Bernie and keeps on talking to Minna barely moving his eyes from her face.

I return with a box of beer, pass them out and sit down while placing the box under the table beside me.

Gunvald is perturbed. He whispers to me, "Green Peace is for pussies." Minna, being the observant lady that she is, turns away from Andy and asks me if I have completed reading *Moby Dick*.

Andy quickly states, "The only good thing that comes out of killing whales is that some fat cat gets a Mercedes Benz. He does not need it. I saw a spout from a whale more than once. They are so fantastic. To kill it and put it into a burger is not right." Who in their right mind would eat a whale burger? God, I promise to only punch him once. Dandy is becoming fired up but notices that the group does not want to get into a Karma draining, useless discussion of conflicting cultures and politics. When meeting guys like this I tell myself to be patient and wait for an opportunity to shut him down with words. If there is a larger party that includes someone like Bernie, let him go first.

Again Bernie gets in there at just the right time. "You want my opinion of whales?"

Gunvald and I reply in unison, "Yes".

"Well, I prefer Scotland."

You have to enjoy and laugh with Bernie's impeccable wit. He is so full of energy and shit.

This morning Minna was looking forty years old. Tonight, she looks twenty-three or twenty-five and beautiful! Katarina also looks good. Everyone does as we all have a glow and having a good time. Dandy boy is feeling uncomfortable because he is not holding court.

We talk about the doggie from yesterday under the umbrella and the hole that he dug by himself in the sand. Bernie says, "I have a cat that visits my garden. It comes and takes a shit in my garden every day. He digs a hole, has a crap and then fills it in."

Most of the table jibe in, "We know cats do that!"

Bernie with his big smile concludes, "Yeah, but with a shovel?"

Sure, it is a cheesy joke but he is on time. The man has true wit. It is late Saturday night and our group is grooving at its best, despite the presence of Dandy Andy.

Our meal arrives hot and tastes superb. I should have tried the food here before. There are no complaints. Talk quiets a little while we eat. Dandy is eating quietly. We eat and a few people make comments on the food. When Dandy Andy tries in vain to resurrect his lecture on Canadian seal hunting, he is ignored. No one at our table acknowledges the dandy.

I usually do not keep track of who pays what when a large group is billed, unless I am asked to. Everyone, except Dandy, puts in enough money to pay for their respective meals and beers brought in from next door. Dandy Andy does not pay for beer or towards a tip. Dandy Andy drinks two beers, at forty Rupees each, after giving me shit about interrupting him in getting them. Yet he only pays for his meal to the Rupee. Enough of Dandy Andy's antics.

Our group leaves for My Dream. Dandy boy decides not to come. Too bad. I will not miss the pencil necked dolt. We arrive at the Dream. Minni, Katarina and Edith sit across the table, facing East. Harry, Gunvald and I sit across from the ladies, facing Charlie's table. Beside Charlie are the English girls playing cards. Paul is among them. Bernie sits at the end of our table, facing the ocean.

Gunvald and I need to stay alert and somewhat sober so we can determine what is going to happen with Charlie tonight. Gunvald is looking intense, alert and on guard.

I cannot resist to give Charlie a look of my pleasant smug smile, showing him how much fun it can be to hang around a great group of people and know that you will have a great time—as long as the group does not let some shit join the ranks for too long of a visit. Charlie and I are sitting at opposite sides of the bar; facing each other down like two men preparing to play chess or perhaps two bullish rams preparing to knock. Do not get me wrong, I would have one hell of a time beating Charlie in a fist fight. It would be a great fight as he is a very tough looking guy who is in very good shape. He reminds me of the great hockey player Mark Messier but not quit as big. I have no fear; the size of the fight in me is huge.

The urge to fight should be kept at bay. You do not fight a guy just because you and your friends may not like the guy, even if he is a true blue asshole. You beat him for assaulting a friend, sexually or otherwise, if democratic justice cannot prevail. The consequences of starting the fight can be devastating. I am not talking about losing the fight either. Criminal charges, jail or worse. You can kill a man with one freakish punch. It is better to remain calm and keep your emotions at bay and save them for when you need them in a situation like we presently have. Reach into the saved emotion when you really need it. Let the adversary take the first punch. Then you have self-defense.

I whisper to Gunvald who remains intense, glancing at Charlie every few minutes, "You seem agitated Gunvald. Let us wait and see what happens. If he insults, we can insult back. I am sure we have the support of our little group as well as the bar manager."

Bernie asks me, "Why are you and Gunvald being so quiet?"

Whispering back, I explain, "Gunvald and I are eying up Charlie. We want to give it to him the moment that he messes around with anyone in our group. We are bloody mad at his antics with Minna last night. He acts like some kind of rapist. Not only was he demeaning, he was bullish and aggressive with Minna. You were there Bernie. Remember when Gunvald and I left you at the boat, asking you to look over Minna?"

"I agree. He is an asshole."

"Then why do you hang around with him?" I ask.

"I don't anymore. He will not get close to Minna again. Do not worry about it anymore. Let it go."

Bernie turns his back to Charlie and sits next to Minna and puts his arm around her. A few minutes elapse when Charlie looks at me from the West side of the bar, I smile at him. He nods his head and states, "It looks like you have yourselves a Knights of the Round Table. Have a good night." Gunvald and I nod at Charlie. Paul gets up from his seat and joins us. He knows where the fun is.

We will not have a problem with Charlie again.

We are now ready for one great party. Bernie starts out hard. He shows us that he can go on for hours telling jokes. Like Minna and Katarina, the more he drinks, the higher pitch in his voice becomes. That is okay.

I walk up to the manager and hand him two thousand five hundred Rupees. I say, "Mr. Manager please let me know where I stand with you from time to time." I hand him four hundred Rupees and say, "This is for letting us stay late." He will have to give the cops' spy at least a couple hundred later. I let our group know that for a few hours swami will cover the tab. It is not an intentional buy of friends but an intentional buy of a great time for all.

Bernie and Harry are folding paper napkins into hats. They look goofy wearing them, as they should. They need bigger napkins.

It is time for some more serious entertainment than silly napkins. "Gunvald, do you want to play table tennis?" I whisper.

"You must be crazy. How?"

"Follow me man." I pick up my cigarette package and hand an unopened one to Gunvald. I then show him how to hold the package between three fingers, his middle finger and thumb so that he can flick his middle finger, with his thumb, against the package to imitate a snapping sound. "The side of the package facing out with the three fingers, is the side that hits the imaginary ball." I whisper to Gunvald and continue to describe how we are going to play.

Gunvald and I move our chairs to opposite lengthwise ends of the table, which is effortless as no one is seated there. I sit down at one end of the table while Gunvald adjusts his chair and sits. I toss the imaginary ball up with my left hand and serve it. I watch intensely as it bounces on the table over to Gunvald. He gazes at the ball and returns it. After a few volleys,

Gunvald really gets into it. When he starts to get a little cocky and aggressive, I smash a sharp return, watch the ball hit fast and fly off the table. Gunvald rubs the imaginary sweat off his forehead and sighs.

Another serve is made and the volley is going. Now the spectators at our table are following the imaginary ball fly from one end of the table to the other, focused in, looking like zombies. They figure the game out quickly. Back and forth, heads turning, following the play. Soon most patrons in the bar are out of their seats and watching the silly fun. We play for ten more minutes, without getting too ridiculous with our shots.

We finish and Edith says, "That was very funny Gunvald and swami. I will have to remember the game. What do you call it?"

"It is called imaginary table tennis in a pub." I reply.

No one asks where the game was learned. They know the answer; from a bar table somewhere in Canada. Bernie and Harry are feeling no pain just now. They look a little dizzy and could not follow the ping pong ball very well.

Later, after some quiet, I announce, "We have here a very interesting table. This evening we have the following from start to finish, A Finnish lady, a Brit from the North and one from the not so far North, a mouthy talkative Canadian, a Norwegian, an Indian, a German lady who is definitely cool and another Finnish lady who is just the right size for me."

Bernie adds, "The international table, from start to Finnish."

We party on and agree that this is probably the best table in India tonight.

It is John's third time in India. He went to Goa for his first two trips. He likes the beach. John is a quiet man. That is why I have not told you too much about the guy. He is nice enough, just quiet and takes it all in. Nothing wrong with that. He is from Jersey, England. A jolly fellow.

John states, "I can see the Irish in you swami. An Irish swami. Your green eyes tell a lot. That is neat."

I reply, "Is that because of the drinking?"

"Not just that, the attitude, the demeanor and the attitude toward life."

I take it as a compliment as Katarina takes half a napkin and leaves for a pee. Reminds me of how Indians joke of Western society being toilet paper people.

John advocates yearly holidays. "Perhaps the government should collect a little more tax and send people each year to a spot, within reason."

"It could be a good idea; a means of rewarding the working poor for their hard work. Unfortunately the rich will not go for it." I stopped myself. Now is not the time for politics. I have almost forgotten about the West. The television channel is not on.

Bernie, feeling a little tight, tells a joke, not worth repeating, of a smelly English woman. He goes on and tells another. "Jesus could not get a job in Jerusalem. He got hammered with tax." The girls are laughing good. Even serious John is chuckling at the bad joke. Some may say this type of humor is almost as bad as saying the Lord's name in vain on a Sunday. Jesus, the historical prophet, would think otherwise and laugh as well.

"Bernie." I call out. "Jesus goes into a hotel, tosses four nails down onto the counter, and asks the room clerk, 'Can you put me up for the night?'"

"You're going to hell swami." Gunvald says.

"See you there buddy." I reply.

I excuse myself and go take a piss in the ocean. It is dark and quiet out here except for the small waves softly covering and then retreating from the flat, wet sand. I am walking back to My Dream and am about twenty feet from the edge of the bar where our table is. Gunvald stands and puts his hand up for me to stop. "Stop for a moment swami, I want to take your picture with your camera." He picks up my camera from the table and snaps my photo.

I return to my seat and ask Gunvald, "Why did you take my picture Gunvald?"

"I had this sudden urge to take your picture."

"Well, thank you. I hope it turns out buddy."

This photo turns out to be mysterious looking. More on that later. *To hell with that Keenan. Take a very slow and good look at the photo that covers this book. What do you see son? Perhaps a little hint. Your paternal grandfather passed away a few hours earlier across the globe.*

To understand the situation of Northern Ireland, Bernie advises, "You must remember the eighteenth century when the British sailed over and kicked the shit out of the Irish. People were starving." Booze and politics do not mix unless it is Election Day. However, I do not mind listening about how much of a prick Oliver Cromwell was, from an Englishman. *Oliver Cromwell, kid, is another example of the evilness of colonial England.*

The drunken Swede who swears at everyone is walking up the beach again. He is bloody nuts. He wears a tattered shirt and pants. He has long messy red hair, is unshaven and staggering. He swears at the staff of Santana's, "You sell poison. You poison the tourists!" About seven of the staff pick up clubs and face him in a threatening manner. The Swede shuts up and staggers off.

What would Katarina do with a drunken swami anyway? It is 7:40 a.m.. I have given up on her long ago. She is not the type to become attracted to a party man, even though he may think that he is deep and a God loving humanist. I feel good. This is India.

International language prevails as the Europeans take turns at making cheers.

Prabhu, the manager, does not seem upset with us drinkers staying on so long. The staff at My Dream are happy, despite being grossly tired. Three-quarters of them are sleeping on tables.

Prahju being pleased with our drunken good behavior starts playing Indian songs with lyrics about a Swami. We all laugh whenever the name 'Swami' heard.

It is nice to see Bernie and Minna together. We are having one hell of a party. The eight of us groove, dancing in the sand. It is now morning and the sun is rising. We continue to drink and smoke. The tab ran out a while ago and we drink at a more moderate pace. More 'Swami' songs are played. We do not understand the words but when the word 'Swami' is heard we all sing along 'Swami'.

We decide to shut it down. I leave first wanting to exercise as it is not good to go to bed without sobering up some after an all night party.

Down the beach are many fishermen and two female tourists, pulling in a very large fishing net to shore. Twenty or more people are singing and pulling. I am asked to join in as I try to walk by unnoticed. It is great exercise. It is intense when you feel the pull of the ocean, wanting to take back the net that is about a hundred yards out. Forty minutes later, the end of the net is finally on shore. There are about twenty large fish and countless one-footers.

I awake by the sounds of an irate person across the way complaining about her room. It is not near as good as being awakened by the sounds of waves reaching the beach. It is noon and the swami feels great. Outside it looks like body surfing is not in the picture; there is little sun with wind and clouds. It is an excellent day for finishing the last pages of Moby Dick or to hang out with Edith and spend a quality afternoon with her.

Sitting at the Velvet Dawn for lunch, I see a young man crawling on the sand between two restaurants. He is badly crippled, with all four limbs twisted at right angles. Someone did this to him intentionally. Birth defects do not result in that. It is clear that his arms and legs were broken and not reset. How could his father be so bloody horrible? He is about thirty years old. I feel such a sickness as my heart pounds. Why would someone want to do this to their son? I am truly in a state of ignorance. What the hell?

A few minutes later, a couple takes a table in front of me. They wave and introduce themselves as George and Julie from England. Julie asks, "Excuse me young man but what is troubling you?"

I tell them about the young man that hobbled by with twisted limbs.

George says that, "The fathers in England during the early nineteen hundreds crippled their sons to make them beg. This way, they received a guaranteed source of income. Quite sickening, I must say. You cannot only blame India for the disfigured young man you just saw. You can also blame my England."

I respond, "So you see a connection between crippling kids in old England and India today. Keep in mind that this young man was about thirty years old."

"Some mothers would blind their daughters at the turn of the nineteenth century." adds Julie. Beggars. Are they worse than us in decency? No. They are certainly worse off in their plight to earn a living. *Humans, as life goes on Keenan, seem to be far more cruel than one may think. Particularly when you seen something like the poor crippled boy. Thank goodness for the majority of good people on this Earth. Do not dwell on the ignorance or evilness of man. Try to understand it. I know that you are a compassionate young boy, even at your age. I see it in you. You are a beautiful person, my son. Do not, ever, forget where you came from and do not forget to be compassionate, to everyone. You may feel hate sometimes, but apex of hate is to want to kill someone. It is not good to hate that much as you will lose your much needed positive energy for a happy existence. It is unfortunate that humanity has failed in many ways but many humans do their best to make our unstable world a better place.*

Julie asks, "What are you writing about swami?"

"Notes about the crippled young man and meeting you two."

"What are you going to do with the notes?" George asks.

"Most likely write a book to my son, Keenan, regarding father-son advice, the Creator and love."

"What will you call it?" George asks.

"I do not know Sir. The story has not ended."

Julie advises, "The novel, *A Woman's India* is a must-read."

"Taken under advisement dear. Where are you two staying?" I ask.

"We are staying at the Padmanabhapuram Palace." says George.

"That cannot be here at Kovolum. You must be visiting the beach on a day trip."

"That is correct. You may have passed it on your way here." States Julie.

I learn that they are here for two weeks and that they do not take Larium but a less hazardous anti-malarial. They take two pills a day. There is a young girl exercising yoga. We talk about yoga and I mention about the yogi that I met a year ago.

"His name was Shirish and he was from Northern India. He was married to a Canadian woman. His wife and he showed me some photos of him doing some most excellent yoga moves. The best one was Shirish doing a one-hand stand with his body in a horizontal position. His right arm was supporting his body, just below his belly button, in a push up position while his legs and left arm extended outwards, reaching out far for the sake of balance. The Himalayan Mountains were in the background."

George gets up from his seat and places his fingers on the table. Julie does not move. Holy lick! George is doing a handstand horizontal on the table using three fingers of each hand. "You have good strength" I say, (left out the part, for an older gentleman), "Good on you man!"

George and Julie pose for a picture and leave after some positive chat.

Gunvald arrives and we leave for lunch to the Lonely Planet.

Gunvald says after we order, "It is becoming redundant here."

"It has been a good party, we should travel."

"Let's try to leave on Monday."

I suggest, "I bet that Edith and Harry would like to get away for a few days. Let's go over to Edith's later and see if she is interested, after we catch some waves and work off lunch."

Gunvald nods with assent with a mouth full of rice and hot pickles. I drink a Raj and eat light.

Gunvald, Edith and I are sitting on the patio outside of Edith's. It is not quite a patio but a wide hallway going around the inner circumference of the complex. The walls are red brick. Edith pours us rum and Pepsi.

Edith asks Gunvald, "Have you traveled anywhere besides India Gunvald?"

"India is my second major trip. My first major trip was to Zimbabwe. I was there for five months. I love the place. I would like to take property and live there."

"Was it safe?" I ask.

He explains that it was, at the time, one of the safest African countries to tour.

"Edith Braun, twenty-five days against the Atlantic. A Swedish woman wrote the book about my unfortunate sailing adventure," Edith says and then hands me a paperback with a yellow cover about an inch thick. Damn, no picture of a youthful Edith on the cover. She would have been bombshell.

"I got bad German press. The popular women from central Germany ruffled their feathers at who they thought was a North German fisherman. I was not a fisherman nor am I a daughter of a fisherman. Not that there is anything wrong with someone who fishes. I like fish. Not as much as I like rum or you swami." She retrieves another bottle from inside and sits down. Edith is looking at me with those soft sensual brown eyes; she radiates mature beauty.

"I made a little money from this little book. I was able to travel a great deal for such a young lady. There was press of me all over the world. I met famous actors and others, the Rolling Stones, Peter O'toole and Paul McCartney," advises Edith. She is not pretentious in her story telling. She is self assured yet humble.

"I got a call from Paul McCartney but I did not know that the Beatles were on top of the record charts. I had hardly heard of them. He had seen my photo in the press. I guess that he was horny for me after seeing my picture. I brushed him off." She tells with a giggle.

"Mick Jagger and I went out on a date. I knew who he was. Well, I knew who he was but not what he was like. He acted like a complete ass. He drove the car, in London, like an idiot. He drank a lot and strutted like he was a peacock. I first met him at a Beatles party in London. I was twenty-six years old at the time and met sliver lips Mick and asked him who he was."

Gunvald says, "Many people do not like Mick Jagger."

I reply, "No doubt. He struts around, like a French wannabe swordsman, with stuffed tights in the eighteenth century. He plays great music and is an excellent entertainer. Perhaps his ego is too big for his tight little britches."

Gunvald states, "What is the difference between Michael Jackson and an ordinary person?" Edith and I look dumbfounded, yet we probably could go on for hours with our own speculative but funny as hell answers. Gunvald answers for us, "The ordinary person wears their underwear inside of their clothes!" He guffaws and smiles.

Edith tells us that she is not money hungry. I pull out a joint and we smoke it. "Don't let Harry know that I have smoked this with you swami. He does not like me to smoke marijuana."

"Of course Edith."

The press or paparazzi, as Edith calls the buggers, met her at her home at 6:00 a.m. one morning. She was hounded with stupid questions. The sort of crap that you would not want to read, unless you are on a crapper and it is the only magazine within reach. Edith eventually became intellectually dead over the adverse attention. She got some dough out of the deal. "I am not a fame monger." she adds.

"No, Edith you are not. Otherwise you would have shaken your bum until you got on the cover of Playboy," I say.

Edith continues, "The boat trip was a quest. I almost drowned. I was rescued by the French navy. After calling May Day, a German cargo boat offered me a lifeboat. I denied it as the waves were ten meters. It was early morning and pitch black out. I threw my dog and they caught her. They screamed, jump, jump, because the boats were twenty meters apart and flailing in the big waves. I had no sleep in six days of the storm. I had wounds on both hands from pulling ropes".

"Wow, Edith." I exclaim.

"I jumped into the ocean after a short time of deliberation. Later, after being offered pills, I requested and received Cognac."

What a lady.

The rescuers thought Edith was crazy for the May Day at night. There was not, however, an answer to her May Day during the day. There was also the issue with the dog. The story is somewhat cloudy. "I would not have jumped without my dog. No jump without my dog," she says.

We are getting a little buzz on. Rum and Pepsi is the fare for our afternoon tea party. Edith continues, "The S.O.S. went in at 2:00 a.m.. I was rescued at 7:00 a.m.. Boats from Europe came. I was rescued on my 26th Birthday."

Harry arrives and Gunvald pours him a drink.

"Peter O'toole in person, is skinny and has watery eyes. Briget Bardot, had pimples all over her face." It is obvious that the rum combined with the pot has hit Edith good.

"I was a little over twenty years old when I left Port Plymouth, England. I did not want to call S.O.S. because I thought I could make it to the islands of Azores. I was close to the Azores, even though I was close to break up, I sailed on."

She tells us that there were no hurricanes in June in that part of the Atlantic for years, except when she boated. Edith is becoming more difficult to understand. The excitement of her telling the story, coupled with some stiff rum, brings on a thick German slur.

Gunvald says, "Friends, cheers to us having a good time."

"Yes, and to Edith and her story." I say while raising my glass.

Edith continues, "There was 110 miles of wind with ten meter waves. I was not in the eye of the storm, but on the outer edge."

Gunvald and I are listening closely, elbows on our knees and ears leaned toward Edith's lips.

"If I were in the eye, I would not be here having a great time with my new friends and you, my dear Harry."

Edith is now way too lit to quote verbatim as her accent has thickened even more. We see a European woman with wide hips and a round bum, not huge but big and good, walk by. "A lot of flesh, a lot of joy." Harry says.

Gunvald jumps in, "A lot to touch, a lot to love!"

Of course, I must give the old Canadian, "The bigger the cushion, the better the pushen."

We laugh hard, including Edith.

The adventure almost did her in. An excellent quest. Unfortunately the boat owner got bad press due to the break up. He did not receive the anticipated marketing spin offs for making the gesture of sponsoring her. The bloody boat owner insured Edith and not the boat! The insurance was one tenth of the cost. The boat goes down and not Edith. Thank goodness, for dear Edith.

Gunvald, Katarina, Minna, Bernie and I are at the Velvet Dawn. Harry and Edith are having a nap, following a late afternoon lunch. Paul is likely playing cards at My Dream. Against my advice, Gunvald and Katarina order fish.

"This is Sunday. They do not fish on Sunday. I saw that they did not catch much fish on Saturday. Do you want to eat Friday's fish?"

Gunvald answers, "It will be fine."

Katarina nods in approval. They both inspected the barracuda and the snapper. The barracuda and snapper are good fish, unless either is caught on Friday and served on Sunday. Minna and Bernie quietly follow my move and order chicken curry.

The smell from the outdoor, fire-heated stove becomes an odor, soon after the fish is put on. It turns out that the snapper turns out to be crapper.

I ask Muriel, "Muriel, what is that stench? I know that the fish is not fresh."

"I will look into it."

Muriel looks in the stove, talks to the manager who gives him a stern look, and returns. "I bet the manager is going to make him feed us a bullshit story you guys."

"Oh come on swami, I know you mean well but we can take care of ourselves," says Gunvald.

Muriel returns to our table and says, "It must be the lobster that the cook just put on the stove."

"Muriel, it is Sunday and the fish are not fresh. You know that."

"The fish will be fine swami."

"Alright Muriel, if you say so."

Bernie, Miina and I eat our chicken curry without hesitation while Gunvald and Katarina are guarded. It is too bad that they buy the bullshit lobster story.

We do not stay long at My Dream as Gunvald and Katarina leave quickly, holding their stomachs, after puking around midnight.

"Good morning, Muriel. The usual please."

"Certainly swami. How was last night's meal?"

"The chicken curry was great. Gunvald and Katarina got sick last night with food poisoning."

"I am deeply sorry swami. I do not eat fish on the weekend either but manager would not let me intervene."

"It is not your fault Muriel. We will not be eating here again for dinner."

We agree that it is the manager's fault for all of this. "Yes, swami Sir, he is indeed an asshole; but this asshole is my boss and I need this job for the time being."

Hypocrites come in all forms. The manager may seem like a hypocrite for serving rotten fish and making us pay for it. He could just be stupid. No, he is money hungry and likely bought the fish at a discount.

I walk along the beach navigating through the vendors. The peddlers or vendors are akin to the hard sell electronics salesman. "*PLEASE LEAVE ME ALONE. GO TO THE TEMPLE AND SAY YOUR PRAYERS,*" I sing out.

"Temple, what temple?"

"*PLEASE DO NOT BOTHER ME JUST NOW. I WANT SOME PEACE, NOT TRADE.*"

He still does not go away, so I do.

Turning around in front of the Velvet Dawn I see the manager looking at me with a slight scowl. He may be pissed at me for not buying one of his stinking fish the night before. Well to hell with him. We will eat next door at the Flamingo later and rub it in his face, hee, hee.

Gunvald, Bernie, Minna, Katarina and I arrive at My Dream. We decide to boycott the Velvet Dawn. John shows up shortly after our arrival. John tells us of the Ku Klux Klan and their relationship with Marlboro. There is the letter "K" on the package when you hold the package upside down. John was on a kibbutz in Israel. He bought some Marly's and was told of the K.K.K.'s ownership of the cigarette company.

More topics arise, such as who killed Kennedy? What happens after death?

Bernie cannot operate the green lighter. It has been passed from person to person with no go. Bernie is seriously trying to make it work. I take it right from Bernie's hand in a quick motion and toss it on the roof. I smile and without saying a word, hand him my red one. The bugger still cannot light it, so I show him how. "Turn it to the side buddy. That way your finger tip escapes the child prevention ring."

Bernie lights his cigarette and says, "Thanks swambat."

"That is the problem with child proof lighters. They are also drunk proof," I joke.

Edith and Harry arrive. Gunvald and I talk with Edith and Harry about the four of us going on a short tour inland. "We need to hire a taxi." Says Edith. "It will not be that expensive if we feed the driver and let him stay in your room with you swami and Gunvald."

"No problem. The least expensive way of travel suits me fine." Gunvald states.

I ask Edith, "How long shall we go for Edith?"

Edith asks Harry, "Can you leave work for five or six days?"

"I am sure that my business partner will have no objection, more clients for her. I have not taken any time off for a long time. It will be nice to leave here and be able to party with the swami and Gunvald."

We discuss plans and details further and agree that we will leave in three days time; the day after the Finnish ladies are set to leave.

The Wake

It is early Monday morning. There is a pain in my heart and I feel the need to call mother. I get out of bed, get dressed quickly and make a beeline to the phone desk in Edith's hotel.

"Hello mom."

"Your father died two nights ago. The last thing he said to me that evening, was that he had suffered enough." Mom is not sad. She too has suffered much. She speaks without emotion while explaining the events before and including father's death.

I start to bawl.

"Sorry mother. Can't talk this moment. I will call you later after I get a hold of myself."

Father did not leave me any words other than to say that he understood that I was very far away and could not be at his bed side. Mother said she will take care of everything, including his ashes. God love her and her strength.

Even though, Keenan, your grandfather was not the perfect father, like myself at times, I have always loved him and love him now. He is my father. I stuck up for him when he was down. I forgave him and have always tried to understand him.

The heartache, I cannot stop crying. I manage to tell the hotel clerk, who is also the telephone attendant, the news of my father's death. He is no longer looking surprised at my demeanor. Keeping a square jaw, tears flowing steadily down my cheeks, I walk away quickly.

Back in my room I splash water on my face, put on the old swim trunks and go where one can be alone with our Creator and my late father. I make it to the beach and then the ocean without having to talk to anyone. Usually, I would skip in the water and dive in. This time I walk into the water solemnly and do not swim until I must. The salty waves splash my face. Swimming out deep into the ocean I begin to cry again. I am about 125 meters out. Bobbing in the waves, treading water, sobbing, for twenty minutes. I do not think that it is the end of Dad's existence. There is no end in my belief system, as energy does not die. Life's energy is everywhere and father is not far away.

I pray. Dear God, my Lord, Mother Nature, the universal God, Mohammad, Allah, our Creator, Brahma, Jehovah and my friend Jesus, please hold my father's hand as you take him into heaven. I pray and know that you forgive him for all the wrong and hurt he caused. He just needed to be loved but did not know how to freely give love or receive it. Even though I believe that heaven is not a 'pie in the sky' and that heaven is here on Earth and beyond, I wish that you take my father to a peaceful and beautiful eternity. If he returns to earth as an animal please make him an eagle. He had a great eye for carpentry so I am sure that he will make a great eagle. Thank you God.

Swimming in one place I pray some more. There's the most beautiful mysterious feeling going through my body just now. It is not just a tingling sensation. I am floating high in the crest of moderate waves. I do not feel my body working to stay above the water as I am almost levitating, dancing within the waves. While I pray for my Dad's soul I thank God and Dad for all the good the world has given me so far—Life. I love you Dad without regret. You do not have to feel guilty about anything that you have done nor regret anything that you did not do. You are free now father.

Selfishly, I ask that his soul touch me thinking that he is receiving my heartfelt request. Then it happens. A burst of energy hits my chest. I feel an energy of love and peace fill my body. The energy of Dad's spirit enters me, not with a thud but with zing while it pushes me back parallel through the crest of a small wave. It is a beautiful feeling. Not just a small tingle you get down your spine when you see a duck and her newborns waddle next to a stream in late spring. It feels euphoric, seemingly close to enlightenment. The feeling of peaceful bliss coupled with enough energy, strength and will power to move mountains, fills every cell in my body. Thank you God. Thank you father for bringing me into this world. I continue treading water and looking at the sky, totally in awe. It is the most intense, cell filling, wonderful experience to feel such energy so intensely.

I swim inland and then swim parallel to the shoreline. The tears have ebbed. I feel sad for Dad's death but also feel thankful that he has entered the next path of life. He will be at peace. I will miss him but know that he will always be with me. I am one half of him. His soul may move on, however, the feeling of his energy entering me remains vibrant. I keep swimming along the shore line, up to My Dream and then circle back to where I entered the water, in front of the Velvet Dawn.

I swim to shore, walking the beach,

Crying, praying,

Looking up to God and the heavens.

Smiling,

I walk for an hour.

One end of the beach to the other.

Thinking about Creation, my father's soul and whether his energy will without a doubt survive.

But I know that Dad is not alone.

Knowing that I am not alone in our wonderful universe,

I thank you Creator for allowing me to know about the energy thing—Love—Mother Nature. I thank you for reminding me that man is only a moment on earth.

I thank you mother and father for wanting a son and trying for a fourth time.

Keenan, I should tell you a little about your late paternal grandfather. He was a great athlete in his time. He twice won the Saskatchewan Provincial Track and Field gold medal for Javelin when he was in grade ten and eleven. I am sure that he would have won a third time, however, Dad did not finish grade twelve until much later. He played fastball in his teen years and early twenties. He was hired out often to different teams who wanted to win badly and pay some money for it. I am told that he could pitch like the mythical Zeus throwing balls of fire. I could not catch his fastballs until I was fourteen years old and even then some of them would knock me right over, with ball in mitt.

Your grandfather, Keenan, was one hell of a hockey player. At age twenty-one, during the regular season, he played in the Carrot River Valley Hockey League. It was a North Saskatchewan hockey league and he played for the Kinistino Tigers for part of the season. He played sixteen games, scored thirty goals and made eighteen assists. That equates to a three-point average per game. That is a very good statistic.

During the next season Dad played for the Blaine Lake Imperials in the same league. He was working in Saskatoon and drove out to the games to play. He was paid well. He played sixteen games, scored thirty-one goals and made thirty-seven assists. That equates to a four-point-two-five average. Amazing stats! He played even better in the Parkland Hockey League a few years later. Again he played sixteen games but scored thirty-two goals and made forty assists. Keenan I will let you figure out the statistics for these games.

My old man was good at a lot of stuff. He taught me how to pound a nail and showed me how to air out a room using the indirect draft method. Cutting the grass, raking the leaves and shoveling the snow were taught early. Dad was an excellent carpenter and shared many of his ideas. My father was also a generous man. People see that and then try to take advantage. I saw that happen to him a few times.

I was proud to stay up late on a Friday night to watch Alfred Hitchcock's movie, 'The Birds'. I was six years old and my older sisters were not allowed to watch it. You see Keenan, I made good coffee and scratched Dad's back better than my sisters at six years of age. Anyway, what I am trying to tell you is that my father was a far better man than certain people thought. Simply because a man has a weakness for booze and women, it does not necessarily make him bad all round. He had a good heart and gave what he could.

The fact that Dad laid lickings on me quite a bit, does not make him a bad person. I forgave him and moved on long ago. Dad knew this. He also knew that I was not a PLOM. Poor Little Old Me. Some things he did to others, I had difficulty forgetting. Like having affairs during his marriage to my mother. She had to put up with a lot of shit and abuse. God love her. At the end of your day, forgiveness is definitely quite a personal thing.

You cannot love, really love, if you cannot forgive. Keenan, your paternal grandfather was a good man.

I am walking on the beach and notice that there are a good number of patrons at My Dream and not many at Santana's. I approach the Velvet Dawn but do not look up, not wanting to see the manager asshole. I see Bernie and Minna seated at the Crab Club. Unbeknownst to me, Bernie and Minna saw me in the ocean mourning and walking the beach. They figured out what happened and decided to leave me be until later. Bernie and Minna are holding hands and look like they are in love.

The tears have dried. I think that there should be an Irish wake this evening, it is better to celebrate a life with friends than to mourn alone.

"Good afternoon Minna and Bernie."

"Hello swami. We saw you walk the beach and swim the ocean. We could see that you heard news of your father's death. Are you okay?" Minna asks.

"Yes. I am now. Thank you."

Bernie, after discussing life, says, "This ain't no dress rehearsal."

"That's right Bernie. You only go around once so make each and every day your best."

"The drum vendors should sell guitars, not cheap drums. The sound of the guitar is more pleasant than the drum." Bernie says.

"Your Henna Tattoos are very nice Minna and Bernie. They are identical. Are you two in love?" I ask.

They both smile and Bernie answers, "We are going to get married some day."

You can tell that they are in love, their holding hands, smiling and giddiness shows. "I am happy for you two. You will work well together."

Minna says that she and Katarina are leaving tomorrow. They are going to end up at the beach North of Madras in about a week. I tell Minna I have to be in Madras around the same time. We decide that Minna will call Kuti and give him the name of the place where they are staying so we could meet up for a short while.

"Minna and Bernie, what do you think about us having an Irish Wake for my father tonight? Nothing fancy, but a small short party with the eight of us celebrating Fred Bittner's life." Bernie states, "I mentioned to

Minna earlier that we should have a party for your father. I am into that. It is a swell idea swami."

Minna asks, "Is an Irish Wake what I think it is? Don't you need a body and a casket?"

Bernie responds, "Not necessarily love. A simple picture will do. Besides, swami will figure that part out."

"Yes, I will Bernie. I will look after the details and ask Edith to help out. Her courtyard will be the perfect place for the wake."

Minna nudges Bernie and whispers into his ear. Bernie says to me, "What do you think about having an engagement party right after the wake."

"That is an excellent idea. Sadness, celebration of life and then celebration of love. When you see Katarina and Paul I am sure that you will let them know of the parties. I do not usually run into Paul during the day. I will go to see Edith and make some plans and purchases."

Bernie says, "I will make sure Paul, Gunvald and Katarina know of the wake."

"Thank you Bernie."

We decide to have a wake for my father at 6:00 p.m. until 8:00 p.m. in Edith's courtyard. The engagement party will start at eight in the evening at the rooftop restaurant. A fabulous mix.

"Will you be our best man?" Bernie asks me.

"Sure thing Bernie. Give me your left hand."

Bernie holds his left hand up with the palm facing me. He knows what is going on. I place my right hand against his left and ensure all the crevices between are fingers are even. I smile. "I knew it Bernie. We have the exact same hands."

"Now you know my ring size swami."

"I will take care of the rings."

"That is cool guys." Minna says.

After sizing Minna up with my pinkie, I get up to leave and put a hundred Rupees on the table for the bottle of water and beer I drank. "No swami, I will get your beer. You paid most of the tab at the big party two nights ago." Bernie says.

"Thanks man."

"Good bye Minna. Good bye Bernie."

"It will be okay swami," says Minna.

"Take care swami." Bernie adds.

"Thank you friends. I will see you in the courtyard at six."

I leave to find Edith and find her sitting outside her room. She sees me and my eyes begin to well up. She knows. She stands up, gives me a big hug and whispers peacefully and lovingly in my ear that it is going to be all right.

She continues, "He has gone on to a beautiful place. It is better to pass on than to suffer in bed with terminal cancer swami."

"I understand. Thank you Edith."

"So what next swami?"

"Edith, I ran into Bernie and Minna at the Crab Club. They saw me on the beach and in the ocean mourning. It is weird. They were also thinking that we should have a party for father. So, when I asked them if they would attend an Irish Wake, they were on the same page as I." Edith is listening intently. "Bernie says that he and Minna are in love and suggest an engagement party at 8:00 p.m., following a two hour wake."

"Those are good ideas swami." Edith says showing concern and compassion. "Where will we have the wake and what do you need?" I tell her of my ideas. She agrees that her courtyard will be a suitable venue for the wake and agrees that Suki's rooftop restaurant is the best choice for the engagement party.

Edith takes me by the hand. We go down to the far end of the beach to shop. We arrive at a store where Edith is acquainted with the owners. She introduces me to two older British hippies who run the place. Edith picks out a ring for Bernie and I find one for Minna. I try them on and they fit. Bernie's is a little snug on my wedding finger while Minna's fits well on my pinkie. They are not expensive, somewhat plain, yet charming. Edith walks over to an earring display and looks at a pair of earrings. She turns to me and smiles, her eyes sparkling.

"Yes, I will buy them for you dear."

"Thank you swami." She hugs me good.

"Edith, let's find a pair of earrings for Katarina so she doesn't feel left out.

"Good idea swami."

We then go to an art store and pick up some masks, candles, incense, stars and moons. I also buy a green picture frame and some brown paper. We return to Edith's room and spread out the artwork on her little table outside her door.

While Edith has a shower, I affix the masks to the pillars using string that Edith found in her closet. They face toward the courtyard. After much difficulty putting tea candles behind three of the masks, I light them. There eyes glow, except for the Hindu looking king as his eyes are solid. I then draw a picture of you father because I do not have a photo of you with me. Not a bad job. Your face is smiling and I make sure that you have a good head of hair, strong jaw lines, hardy looking forehead and broad shoulders. I put the drawing in the green frame and write Fred Leo Bittner, born in July and passed on in January, in his sixty-fourth year. I place the picture on the wide ledge, facing the courtyard, between the masks and pillars.

Do I ever I miss you Dad. I regret my absence from you during your last day in the hospital. But why did you decide to die now? That is a selfish remark on my part but oh the pain. Or is it guilt for not making a good effort to return to Canada? I could not come back. Even if I would have given more than a hundred percent effort, I know it could not have been done financially. The guilt derives from past experiences of reading a book or watching a movie that has the oldest son at the bedside of his dying father. Are they there under obligation or for inheritance? To hell with the melancholy of *War and Peace*. Furthermore, sometimes in life you know a result beforehand. One should not feel guilty for being able to KNOW. I would not have made it in time and this beach is where I should be. I am at peace with you now my father. No PLOM here Fritz. Let's have one hell of a party for you, my dear Dad.

Father, the sketch of you is my depiction of the photo of us when we were at Crooked Lake together. The one where I am just shy of being four years old and you are carrying me up on your shoulder around the beach.

It is spring. You can see that I am happy. I can see that you are proud, proud to finally have your son.

I stack three packages of cigarettes on the ledge beside the picture. Next to the cigarettes lay a deck of cards; Dad sure liked to play cards. I light some candles and put them on the right hand side of the picture. The make shift shrine for the wake is almost complete. I hang three moons and three stars from a line strung between the two pillars. They are small but add a spiritual effect to this little universe. A Zen Buddha sits on the ledge to the right, looking at the picture.

We have some Hinduism and Buddhism represented here, along with life, love and remembrance. One may think that a crucifix should be present as it is an Irish tradition at a wake. Number one, Dad was not Irish. Two, we are not in Ireland or North America. Three, this is my show for my father and we are in India. Lastly, I do not like the crucifix. *You Keenan, already know why and understand this.* For other readers, it has much to do with the crucifix's part in the oppression, repression and suppression of modern man.

I step back and take a look. The shrine exudes energy. The sun has set fully and it is now dark. The masks are glowing and I am content with this shrine. In fact, I am proud. Smiling to myself, I feel that it is a job well done and that I am doing the right thing. I am sure Dad would have wanted me to do this. Not a big piss up but a respectful little party. Even though Dad was not Irish and I just part Irish, a wake is the right way to go. In addition, Dad acted more Irish than German or Montana Sioux. Besides, I had to do something honorable.

Edith comes out of her room and pours herself and me a rum and Pepsi. She hands the drink over the ledge to me. I taste it. "You sure make a nice rum and Pepsi Edith. I tend to make them too strong at times."

"Your shrine looks very good swami." Edith walks along the corridor, into the courtyard and approaches the shrine from the front.

"Oh, the masks and candles look great."

Taking a closer look, Edith looks at the drawing of father and says, "Did your father really look like that? He is very handsome."

"He was a good looking man. Perhaps the jaws are wider than actual. But close."

"Was his hair that curly?"

"No, it was a wavy curl but he wore it short and slicked it back with hair cream. I must say that the sketch somewhat looks like a cartoon, however, it depicts what I remember of my father. Good looking, strong and a good heart, deep down."

"That is good."

"What time is it Edith?"

"It is almost 6:00 p.m.."

"Perfect, let's make sure that we have enough rum and Pepsi."

Gunvald arrives and sees the shrine. "Great job swami. Looks good." He pats me on the shoulder and gives me a hug. The three of us take glasses from Edith's room and set them out on the round table in the courtyard. The sky is clear, allowing the stars to shine freely below with glowing brightness. I turn around and look at the shrine. It looks entrancing and quite spiritual. Minna, Katarina and Bernie walk into the courtyard with a bottle of rum and a bag of Pepsi. We sit around the table and pour some drinks. Harry and Paul have yet to arrive.

"Excuse me, swami." Gunvald takes my camera from the table and states, "Why don't you go over to your father's shrine for a photo." Shit, I do not even have a shirt with me. At least I take my hat off.

Paul arrives and then Harry. Everyone in our group is here. Bernie, Gunvald and Paul must think that this is a hippy wake as the three of them are wearing tie dyed shirts—groovy. We talk in groups and at large.

The wake's atmosphere is electric. Suddenly a tall skinny pale man walks into the courtyard. He walks up to Edith, takes a seat and starts talking to her. He is talking unclearly but I make out that he would not kill a person for his country. He yells about some Indians wanting to kill him. He obviously has done L.S.D. a few too many times. He does not understand the reason for our gathering. Apparently the acid messed him up. Edith knows the story. He got scared and freaked out. He is really crazy in the head. He is very paranoid about the Indians. Why be in India then shithead? Maybe it is because he is so pale. I take his picture after Edith introduces him. He continues his rant, preventing conversation for the rest of the table. Enough of the German's antics, it is time to act.

"Do you know what you are doing here Sir?" I ask Hans sternly. "You are crashing my father's wake. He died the other night and we are celebrating his life. If you are going to stay please respect this event and keep your voice down. Your loud screechy voice makes me cringe. When I cringe, I get angry. Believe me Hans, never make a man angry at a funeral or wake. You could end up dying yourself."

He replies with, "I am sorry."

Paul is rolling a reefer in hopes of calming Hans down. It works. He does not talk as loud and the panic appears to leave him.

Keenan, in a conversation try to add to it. Do not interject unless absolutely necessary. Ensure that the question or statement affects or entertains more than one person if you are in a group this size or larger. Do not hold court for too long, like a Dandy Andy. If one person in your group is crazy, be patient, try to understand the nut and provide him with some firm direction. If you are hosting the party and there is an agenda do not hesitate in getting things started and stay the course.

"You know, I will never see father again, his body. So I will take a photo of his sketch."

Bernie states, "It will be a good photo, because you have ashes in the ashtray next to the picture."

"I agree Bernie."

Minna asks, "Tell us about your father swami."

I briefly describe dad's successes in sports, where he came from and how he became at peace with himself after he was told that he had cancer of the lymph nodes that originated in his lung. His excellence at carpentry is also described. I finish off by saying, "He had great eyes for lines and curves. He made no mistake when building a house. Everything was in line exactly. He was a perfectionist. He could read the line on a putting green like Jack. He also liked curves, especially the curves on a woman."

"Your father sounds like he was great at many things." Gunvald says.

"He was a man's man, was he swami?" Bernie asks.

"Oh yeah, and then some. Bernie and Minna, please let me get a picture of you love birds before I forget." They embrace and kiss. They are totally in love, which is a wonderful thing to witness. They make a good couple. I hope that they will be together for decades.

All I know about wakes is that you get together with family and friends to celebrate the deceased's life and have a party. There should be some formal sign of respect, however, so I pick up the sketch of Dad and give it to Minna and Bernie. I do not have to say anything as they pose with the sketch smiling seriously.

Mr. Shopkeeper shows up to take our Pepsi order. He was advised of the wake earlier and his presence is welcomed. Bernie hands him the sketch of Dad for a picture. It is great that he understands, despite the moderate language barrier. He tries hard and that is the main thing. He is a very nice man, who goes out of his way to help a customer. He really appreciates the two shirts that I gave him the other day and thanks me again.

Harry is next. He props the frame up on the tips of his fingers, with the top of the frame balanced and strikes a solemn look. He is also serious and his expression is not contrived. My friends did not know Dad but only a few stories of his life. There is no protocol on wakes or emotional expression at such events. My friends are here to support me and contribute to the wake. That alone is enough.

Turns out Gunvald is a pro at mourning and paying respect to the recently deceased. Gunvald changes his shirt before I take his picture with father. He takes the wake seriously and holds the sketch of dad with importance. He does not have to muster up a solemn face because he takes the moments to heart. Gunvald is not acting here. Not only is Gunvald sad for me he is also sad that father had to die before his retirement years.

Katarina poses with the sketch. Then the picture passes to Edith and then Paul. Paul is having a good time. He has been to Irish wakes before. Even crazy Hans wants his picture taken with father.

I take the sketch of who we now call 'Daddy' and place a few drops of rum on his head from the cap. Gunvald blesses him with gin. Everyone in the knight's roundtable is genuine, compassionate and caring. It is an excellent wake with ample respect. I bless Daddy with incense. Gunvald goes to town and blesses him with marijuana smoke.

Paul stands and announces, "Let us have a toast. Let us have a big toast to the evening trilogy, to a wake, a wedding and a full moon in India." We raise our glasses and exchange a few international cheers.

"A VEDDY GOOD TOAST PAUL. VEDDY GOOD." I say.

Gunvald prefers one on one talk over group discussions. Cocktail conversation can be boring unless you have the right people present. There are not any egomaniacs at this table, except for a crazy Hans, who is hopefully just passing by. Our group of eight is simply great.

Katarina tries her best to tell Gunvald and I more of herself. Her grandfather was a Jew and her grandmother a Cossack, on her father's side. Her mother is one hundred percent Finnish. There are only ten people alive in her family with the same last name. There is also talk about decedents from a Chinese town with Katarina being the last one, a great show and a Mongolian riding a horse. I sure wish I could understand the whole story and listen to it in more detail some sober time later; it seems so interesting. I do not know much about Finnish history and the inter-relationship between Russia, Mongolia and China during the eighteenth and nineteenth centuries. Keenan, you figure it out if you want.

I tell Katarina, "So Katarina, you should take a husband who will, without regret, take your last name."

Ghoulish Hans starts to get excited again.

Edith comes over and whispers to in my ear, "I know that he is a bit of a pain in the ass but he is from the same German town as me." Oh shit he is leaving. It is so sad to see him leave. Not!

"Look Edith, Hans is leaving." I whisper back to her and blow subtly in her ear, causing her to giggle.

Katarina says that the happy couple must have one child for each of us six, and name them after each of us. She says, "It will be Harry, Edith, Paul, Katarina, Gunvald and swami."

"Do you think that we can make that many babies Minna?" Bernie asks with a big grin.

"No way." She replies.

After a pause Gunvald states that friends of his carry pepper spray for protection. It is difficult to grasp because Oslo is not known to be violent. You do not hear about it. Maybe they are some radicals in Norway like most everywhere. "Are there skin heads in Norway, Gunvald?" I ask.

"Not the Nazi types that you hear about on CNN in Germany, just radical anarchists who despise authority."

Harry pulls out a good bottle of rum that he says that he bought in Trivandrum. He opens the bottle and pours us a drink. It is good strong dark rum.

"Nothing, I do nothing." Paul says in response to Gunvald asking him what he does. His response reminds me of a *Seinfeld* episode regarding nothing. It is obvious that Paul does not want to get into work talk. Paul is an interesting man.

Paul lights up a large reefer, takes three puffs and passes it across the table to me. Gunvald, teaching me his trick, the funny boy … after I pass him the fat joint, he tokes three times and thinking he will pass it back to me, before it goes on its never-ending journey around the table, I look and he goes left. That is counterclockwise you bugger, you are supposed to take two puffs and pass the joint to the right. This is too funny. I am not a hard ass nor is pot expensive here but just a stickler for pot smoking etiquette. Gunvald passes it to Paul and stands there and waits. He then takes it back and passes the joint to Minna. He then gets up and goes and talks to Minna and Bernie. He is sitting there and smirks while Bernie takes two puffs and hands him the joint. Gunvald hands the joint back to Bernie, he takes a puff and hands it over to Paul.

I say, "Okay friends. Instead of musical chairs why don't we play musical reefer?" *Hey kid, I had to say it.*

Gunvald stands and walks over to and sits in the empty chair that Hans recently sat in. No joke, he takes the reefer and has a good two pulls. The stick is grinning ear to ear. He sees that I have had enough and comes over and sits beside me.

"Got you going swami."

"Sure did buddy. Your new nickname is now chopsticks. Do you like it?"

"No. I want something better."

"All right. I will think of one and report to you on our inland trip."

Harry calls Katarini Macararina by error and Katarina offers with a giggle, "A dear child has many names."

Gunvald tells us that he spent much time a few years ago in Zimbabwe. When he was in a cave he took a photo of the moon through the opening in cave when he was loaded. The photos turned out black. "I strongly believe that the first humans were in Africa" he says.

I reply, "Gunvald, India also has an ancient race in the Hindus Valley. Anyway, we must go to Africa Gunvald. I want to see a lion."

Gunvald says, "If you smoke filters you will not last long swami."

Bernie jumps in, "My dad smoked and had drinks until he was quite old. He had a third of whiskey every day. He was happy all the time. He lived until he was seventy-eight years of age."

"That's what I like to hear Bernie. Escape the cancer by not being afraid of your liver running away from you."

"You are crazy swami." Minna states.

Paul reminds me of Phil Collins somewhat. He is better looking than Collins and has a tough strong masculinity to him. He brings up the movie *Midnight Express*. Six out of eight of us have seen it. "The scenes are vivid," Paul says. "It is a classic prison movie."

"It is intense when the main character kills that guard by smashing his body and neck against the wall and coat hook." I add.

Edith says, "Oliver Stone does a great job at drawing the audience to feel sorry for Davis when he is being questioned by the police after they find the hash."

"I did not feel sorry for the spoiled brat." Gunvald states. "He arrogantly tapes hash to his body and fills his boots too. He tells his father that he did it for the money. There is no worthy cause. You do feel sorry for him when he is beaten in prison and ends up with a life sentence."

"It reminds me that there is good reason to respect the laws of the land you visit." I say.

"I do not like unhappy dark movies. Let's change the subject." Minna softly says.

Edith looks at her watch and points out, "It is 8:00 p.m. and time to go upstairs to the restaurant for the engagement party."

Bernie and Minna are gleaming.

"Let's clean up here first so we do not have to do it later." Katarina suggests.

"Thank you Katarina. Good idea." says Edith. "Please leave the empty bottles neatly under the table. The staff will retrieve them." We all pitch in and less than two minutes later we are walking up the stairs to the restaurant.

Suku's Roof Top Restaurant is medium sized. It sits two stories up with a view from the outer five-foot walls. There are partitions made of bamboo. It is beach-like, similar to the restaurants on the sand, yet it has a sense of class to it. It has a more Indian feel. We are removed from the busyness of people walking by at the beach level restaurants. The background music furthers the peaceful atmosphere. Suku is not here. His partner Hudi is.

Katarina takes a photo of the best man with the rings. Bernie states hopefully in my direction, "You are putting your good Karma on the rings swami?"

"Yes brother."

Someone lights a cigarette from one of the candles. Minna advises, "Take a light from a candle and you kill a fisherman."

"I thought it was a witch that is killed." I ask and then move Daddy, which one can admit is a corny name, to the next table due to space. He will enjoy watching us all. Someone may think it a bit childish to carry a sketch of Daddy around. What gives a critic clout over the correct way of mourning your own father? *Well son, they can kiss my ass. No more self doubt. For now on I am going to live my life according to what I know is right, not dwell on other peoples negative shit, and harness the universe's energy and realize what I yearn for.*

Bernie pulls out a tie from his bag and puts it around my neck and says, "Since you are shirtless for this formal party, you need to be dressed correctly. The tie will take peoples' gazes from your chunky tummy swami."

"Laugh it up funny boy Bernie." I say.

"Bernie, swami has a nice body. He may have a wee bit of a tummy but Canadian beer is just so damned good." Edith says while looking at me.

Paul adds, "The beer here is as good as anywhere. That's one thing about beer. Even poor nations come up with good beer. Not only our Raj and Kingfisher here but Mexico's Corona is also very good beer."

Bernie says, "This is the best meal this year, it is excellent. The atmosphere is great, the mood is marvelous and we are a fantastic group."

I add, "I do not know why we have not yet eaten here before. This food is so damned good."

Katarina states, while looking at the sketch of Daddy at the next table, "The Daddy picture is better than an actual photo because it comes from his son. I used to love showing my father affection through pictures from school in my early years. I also really enjoyed hosting tea and birthday parties. My mother enjoyed attending my parties."

Bernie chirps, "She would be a good mother-in-law."

A photo of the moon is taken. Harry gets fired up and says, "Let's get a little crazy. Not with that green stuff though. Not for me. It makes me tired and slows me down. That is why you can't get a house built here quickly. The laborers all must smoke the weed."

"Hawhoooooooooh. Hawhooooooooh. I used to be a coyote but I am all right Nowhoooooooooooh." I roar.

"Whoop, whoop, whoop." Gunvald yelps.

"*BOOOOOOOOOOOOO HAAAAAAAAAAA. WHAT THE HELL ARE YOU DOING HUDI? WE NEED A BOTTLE OF RUM AND AN ARM-LOAD OF BEERS.*" Hudi nods and smiles our way while I get up and do a little jig beside the table. "*COME ON HARRY BUDDY. LET'S GET CRAZY.*" After the laughter subsides Harry states, "I, like most Indians, do not dance swami. We like to drink and have sex."

"I get much sex Harry. Too bad half the time swami does not have a partner."

"The charter people come here." Says Paul. "Did you see them arrive today? Don't they look white?"

"Sun-tanning the Gunvald." I laugh. We all laugh big time. Gunvald is snorting, while Harry, Bernie, and Paul hold their stomachs. Tears of joy appear and much laughter erupts around the table. This has to be our biggest laugh. Gunvald is almost pissing himself laughing.

Paul sees me writing furiously just now and says, "swami!" He continues with a chant.

"swami wake."

"swami tour."

"swami for my son!"

The table claps and I take a quick and subtle bow. The fact that Bernie and I have the exact same hand size comes to mind. It is time to determine whether the rest of the men match.

"Gunvald, show me your hand. I want to see if we have the same hand size."

Bernie states, "Good idea swami. Did you tell our group about us finding out that we have the same hand size when we sized up our hands so you could determine my ring size?"

"No Bernie. Thank you."

Gunvald places his left hand against my right. "Exact match swami. That is a little weird."

Paul and Harry's also match.

"Well, fellas, not only do we get along like brothers, we have the same hand size. Isn't that interesting?"

The girls giggle.

Katarina rings a glass. We join in except for Minna and Bernie. They kiss. Total group adulation. We party so well together as there are no leaders, followers, only those who suggest. Unbelievable. Beautiful. As a scientist type would put it, the group dynamics are superb. *Keenan, this is the best party group of people your old man has ever experienced. Not one negative or self-congratulating comment from anyone. It is a true celebration of Life and Love.*

"Excellent food." Katarina says.

Gunvald has finished eating rather quickly and is smoking one of Daddy's cigarettes. "You prefer the sacrificial cigarettes over your poor man's, don't you Gunvald?" He lets out his usual grunt and laughs.

Gunvald says, "Fred's cigarettes are not sacrificed until they turn to ash."

"Good one Gunvald." Says Harry.

Bernie asks me, "I bet this is a lot better than being back home in Saskatchewan right now swami?"

"No doubt. In this case it is better to celebrate a life with friends than to mourn a death with family."

"Where there is a will, there is a relative." Laughter erupts at Bernie's wit.

Edith stands and says, "I would like to make a toast to swami's father. To a great dancer, athlete and carpenter. May you last forever through your blood line."

"Edith, thank you. That was very good." I say and then clap. The rest of the table applauds. "I want to thank you, my new friends, for your support and participation in the wake. With death there is life. Let us now celebrate life and possibly new life through this engagement party."

Gunvald does an African toast and we celebrate Bernie and Minna.

Gunvald holds up Daddy and Harry gives a toast to him, "Here, I toast to Fred Bittner with this new beer."

"Too much head in that beer." Paul says.

Bernie replies, "You cannot ever have too much."

With dinner complete and the dishes taken away, suddenly and deliberately, Bernie stands up, gets down on his right knee and proposes to Minna in his best British accented words, "Will you marry me my love?"

Minna hesitates. The six of us onlookers are quiet and wait. Two seconds pass. Minna then says, "Yes, Bernie, I will marry you." We stand, clap and do cheers to the engaged couple.

I take the pair of earrings out of my pouch and give them to Katarina. She gives me a hug and kiss on the cheek and says, "Thank you for the earrings swarmi." Huh, I think—swarmi? What the heck? Katarina knows it is swami and not swarmi. She does not look that intoxicated, maybe just a slip of the tongue. Speaking of tongues, I would really like to ... No swami. Do not go there.

"Hey swami, anything for me?" Gunvald asks.

"How about another beer?" I reply.

"Sure, that will do. Plus one of the sacrificial filters please."

"You are too funny frenchy. We might as well sacrifice all the cigarettes here."

The Finnish girls are about to leave so they can pack and get some rest as they are leaving early tomorrow. Bernie and Paul are standing. There is a touch of sadness building. There are hugs all the way around. It takes a few minutes for us to say good night and best fortune to all.

Edith, Harry, Gunvald and I remain. A young lady with nice, long legs and a pretty face arrives. Edith introduces her to Gunvald and I. Her name is Helen. Gunvald's eyes are on her. We smoke one with her. Too bad for Gunvald; she too is leaving tomorrow. Edith brings up our tour and explains where we ought to go. The three of us guys talk about having a party in the back seat of the taxi.

It is another beautiful morning in Kovalam Beach. The sky is clear without a cloud as far as I can see. It is hot and I will need to spend most of the day in and near the ocean, like everyday here. Minna and Katarina have left this morning. You cannot see much of India if you stay in one spot for too long. They plan to visit some inland tourist sites and end up at Mamallapuram, Tamil Nadu, which is a small beach artesian destination, nestled in a fishing village North of Madras. The Finnish ladies will phone Kuti and tell him the name of the hotel where they will be staying. My spirits are up while walking the length of the beach, thinking about yesterday. It was one hell of a day.

Yes, my favorite chair at the Velvet Dawn is free. "Good morning swami." Muriel welcomes me. "The usual tea and toast for you?" Despite our boycott of the place, it is worth crossing the picket line and enjoy the hot tea and warm toast. Muriel is a pleasant, short on talk, morning person. He gives you much needed morning space and does not talk your head off.

"Yes Murial. You can't go wrong with tea and toast. Manager not here yet?"

"No, and I hope that he does not come in today. It is his planned day off."

"Well, then you get to run the whole show."

"Yes."

Muriel works and saves hard. He is taking computer courses part time and is saving up to go to university full time. He can't wait to leave work at the Velvet Dawn and his asshole manager boss. Give a person a little bit of power and they may abuse it. Once an asshole, always an asshole. As Fred used to say, "Give a man a two bit job and a fifty dollar suit and they think they have the world by the nuts."

The ocean is good today. There is a slight breeze and the waves are just right. I catch a good one and ride it all the way in. Gunvald really likes to body surf also. It is a great way to spend the afternoon.

I am sitting on my towel, feeling the sun's rays beat on the droplets of water on my arm, slowly evaporating. There are not any insects around. They must be in the shade. The wind is also having a rest. The sun never rests. Matter cannot rest. I am now totally dry, except for my forehead where beads of sweat form and trickle down my face. Life is good.

"Hello swami!" It is Gunvald coming down the beach. I wave.

"How are you doing brother?" He asks with exuberance.

"Great."

"I see that you could use a swim. Where is Daddy?"

"He is in the room. I just got back from a swim and surf but can go back in anytime."

"Well, let's go get Daddy. He will have more fun looking at women walk by on the beach than sitting in your room."

"I agree. We can smoke one there at the same time."

"You read my mind swami."

"Yeah. Yeah." We make our way to my room.

"Let's stop at the corner stand and get a couple of waters. Too early for beer." I suggest.

"Good morning Sir, or is it noon yet?"

Corner stand vendor guy replies, whose name we keep forgetting is Etthuka, "It is just after twelve noon swami Sir."

"Thank you. And thank you again for looking after us with the Pepsi last night."

"You are most welcome swami."

The death of a loved one invariably leads one to dwell on human life and it's place within the vast universe. A stranger's death can also have an effect on you if there is a connection. Gunvald impresses me with his positive attitude and connection to Daddy.

Here we are, the three of us sitting on the beach in front of the Sunset Restaurant, two-thirds of the way to the water. There are no umbrellas or other obstructions in front of us, only a passerby now and then. There are a few sunbathers but no boobies for Gunvald to look at. That is okay because Gunvald and I are about to have a good bullshit session. Daddy stands in front of our towels facing the ocean.

"What would you tell your son about what you believe spiritually and why you believe it?" asks Gunvald.

"Well that is one of the underlying themes of the book Gunvald. Love life, your Creator God and your neighbor. Help fellow man and keep good Karma. Respect nature and love it. I believe in God because I feel God's energy. To love Creation and the Creator, is a form of faith that does not need a religion or religious support. We should stand in awe of the Creation of the universe and appreciate the mystery of her laws. Man does not deserve to know all the answers. Religion desperately fails to fill in the gap. Gunvald I tell you brother, what better place to feel, ponder and embrace the energy our universe beholds, than magical India."

"I agree with what you said. Just because you can't see God's energy does not mean you cannot feel it and know that it exists. Anything else spiritual? What about your experience yesterday when you heard that Daddy passed away?"

"I believe that during one's life, the body and soul are one, not two separate things. At death our soul or Karma changes into a new form of energy and escapes the no longer needed body. When I was in the ocean swimming and praying to God and father I felt father's soul hit me in the chest with a burst of energy."

"Wow swami. Fascinating stuff. It is amazing and exciting to be with you right now and experience part of your story."

"Gunvald, my friend, with all my heart I thank you for being here."

"What would you say to your son about your chosen profession?" He asks.

"I would say, 'Keenan, being a lawyer means being held to a higher standard which is stressful and often difficult. You cannot tell a pain in the ass client to go to hell. A plumber could tell him to go to hell but I cannot. The client would call the law society and I would be punished, penalized and paved over with paperwork. In addition, the legal profession tends to attract more assholes than other professions; those who want big money and power. I understand that it is a broad generalization, however, the reputations of lawyers in the West are worse than prostitutes and used car salesmen. The generalization is an unfortunate one as most lawyers I know are good people'."

Gunvald and I are swimming and body surfing. Looking toward our space on the beach, I see a sexy older woman, about fifty-three years old, stop by Daddy. She crouches down and takes a close look at him. I want to know her story and check out her body so I move quickly through the waves and walk briskly to her.

"Good afternoon my dear. I suppose you are wondering about the sketch."

"Yes I am. Who is Fred Bittner?"

"He is my father who passed away three days ago in Canada."

"I am sorry to hear that. Why the sketch?"

"We had a wonderful Irish Wake for him and I did not have a photograph or his body so I had to draw him."

"You are a good son for doing that."

I would ask her name and flirt with her but damn it, she is wearing a wedding ring.

It is around 4:00 o'clock in the afternoon and Gunvald takes Daddy into the room for a nap at my request. It is a good thing because a few people are beginning to look at us strangely. Gunvald wisely reminds me to give Daddy a drink of beer. After shaking a golden drop on his head he leaves with Gunvald. He returns and says that Daddy looks happier. Gunvald is cool, intelligent and caring.

I say to Gunvald, "It is too bad that father never walked India. Too bad that he did not travel much at all. A trip to Las Vegas by car may have had something to do with it. Part of the trip turned out awful for my parents. They found a pipe bomb under a lamp shade. They could not figure out how to turn on the bedside lamp when they got into their hotel room. This was during a time when some casino owners were after each other. Mom looked under the light shade and found a pipe bomb. The police came and took the bomb and blew it up in the desert. My folks left Vegas that night."

"That is a good thing swami, that your mother found the bomb and that the switch did not turn on the lamp."

"Yes Gunvald. It would have been utterly devastating to lose both parents at once."

Gunvald and I decide to return to Suku's rooftop restaurant for dinner and meet at the Velvet Dawn right after sunset. The cool shower is refreshing. I wash some clothes in the shower using hand soap and hang them across the makeshift string of a clothesline across the room.

Suku and Hudi serve the best food on the beach, if not in all of Kerala. Suku has carved up an onion and tomato to make a rooster. We take a photo of Daddy and the rooster made of onion, tomato and carrot. Cook Suku is said to be the number two guy in Kovalum Beach. Gunvald and I wonder if the number one guy actually exists. Hudi made last night's meal. Gunvald and I decide to order. Tonight we have both Suku and Hudi. We think they are more than business partners, not that there is anything wrong with that. They are both good looking guys, but the hair, big, black, shiny hair. They do not look overly queer but the hair makes them look like fancy boys.

Gunvald and I order curried chicken, a vegetable dish and rice. We forgo rum and order beer instead.

There is Kathakari happening around the corner on the hotel patio. It is Indian dancing and mime at its best. It is really cool as his face is stone like. To be a Kathakari performer takes years of training. It is a dance drama that is unique to Kerala and can go on for hours. Gunvald and I watch for some time.

Daddy views the kitchen and meal. He is good company; he does not talk too much. Gunvald states, "Daddy appears to be floating, blowing out air, floating but a still picture." He does. "Gunvald, do you actually think the picture is changing or is it us and our psyches?"

"A little of both perhaps. The picture will change over time with sunlight fading the ink on the page, in addition to us putting beer droplet offerings on it. Our perception of Daddy changes as time passes and the news of his death becomes less saddening."

"Gunvald, I am going to have to start calling you Swami Gunni."

"Sounds good swami, better than chopstick."

During this short discussion our eyes have not left Daddy for more than a moment.

Turns out that a middle-aged man from a couple tables over, thinks Gunvald and I to be looney. We are listening to nice Mantras during our meal. I noticed him staring at us before. He walks by us and says, "You are lost." He then marches by to go to the washroom. He returns and I quickly stand up, block and face him.

"Excuse me Sir, why do you think we are lost?"

"Because, you are two grown men talking to a picture. You look crazy for worshiping some kind of idol."

I respond assertively, "We are certainly not. See here." I point to the picture. "This is my father. He died in Canada three days ago. I am mourning him and my good friend here is supporting me. Is that okay with you Sir?"

"I understand. I am sorry. What is your name?"

"My name is swami. What is your name? I like to know the name of the man I am about to punch in the head."

"Ati. Please do not hit me. A strong man like you could hurt me badly. I am truly sorry."

"Well Ati, if you are so sorry, why don't you buy my friend and me a beer?"

He does.

"That was excellent swami." Gunvald is gleaming. "And you got us beer out of it!"

"I can understand that we may have looked weird but all he had to do was come over, excuse himself, and ask us what we were doing. Some people would not have been so kind to him."

"We can still kick his ass if you want."

"No Gunvald, having him look and feel like a fool is enough. We do not need the negative Karma either."

"Don't forget the beer. There is satisfaction when a man buys a beer for a stranger after he realizes that he screwed up."

"Yes the beer. You know Gunvald, it will be good to leave here. It is almost too much to be on a beach partying for more than ten days. We would be fat if we did not swim so much."

"Like I said before swami, it can get redundant if you stay at a place for too long. When you travel you should travel. To stay in one place when traveling is not natural. I have stayed this long because of you and the rest of our group."

"I agree Gunvald. There is so much more of India to experience. Thank you for your support and friendship."

We do not stay on long; we have a big day tomorrow. We need rest from all this enjoyment. *On a personal note, Keenan, I need to let things sink in and finish up some notes of what has happened. There is some very powerful stuff going on inside me and the recent events need to be put into perspective. Experiencing such energy from the supernatural is something else.*

The Tour

"Good morning my dear Edith. It looks like you are all ready to go." She gives me a hug.

"I packed last night. You can put your suitcase and boxes in the closet. Put Daddy on the shelf there. We can lock up and meet Harry and Gunvald in front of the hotel. Harry is already there with our bags."

"Thank you Edith." It is time to stop carrying Daddy around. The picture will be treasured always as it represents all the positive things he has done.

"Good morning Harry. Excited about our trip?"

"Yes swami. It is going to be a good day to travel. Let me introduce to you our taxi driver."

Holy lick! He must be the long lost son of Sammy Davis Jr..

Harry continues, "This is Vinesh. Vinesh, this is swami."

We shake hands. *"PLEASED TO MEET YOU VINESH. WHAT THE HELL? DO YOU KNOW THAT YOU LOOK JUST LIKE THE GREAT SINGER AND COMIC SAMMY DAVIS JUNIOR? I AM GOING TO CALL YOU SAMMY. ARE YOU OKAY WITH THAT YOUNG MAN?"* I ask with a serious face fighting hard against the smirk and laughter that wants to burst out.

Harry and Sammy are laughing.

"You can call me Sammy Mr. swami."

Harry asks, "Who is Sammy Davis Junior?"

Edith answers, "He sang with Dean Martin and Frank Sinatra. The three of them are known as The Rat Pack."

"That's right Edith. Dean Martin and Sammy Davis Junior are the best. It is an honor to be called Sammy."

Gunvald arrives and spunky Sammy finishes loading the trunk. Sammy lives in Kovalam. It is easy to be put in a good mood with a smile like his.

Our first stop is the Periyar Tiger Reserve. Sammy likes the nickname regardless of whether he can understand it or not. Sammy says, "Sammy and swami cousins." Edith laughs while sitting in the front passenger seat with us three men in the back of the black shiny, four door, smallish sedan. The roof is curved so if you are not in the middle and next to the window, you have to either crook your neck to the side or slouch. That is okay, the company is great and Sammy fits right in. Harry and I leave our windows open so we can put our arms out to make room. Gunvald, the stick, takes the middle and sits erect. I do not like sitting in the middle of two men. Woman are another story. You can put your arms around them, unless they are as big as a house, like a certain golfer we know.

Sammy pulls up to Periyar House, home of the Periyar Wild Life Sanctuary. The hotel complex looks impressive. The rooms are expensive at almost a thousand rupees a night. The meals are cheaper. I go out and buy beers for Gunvald, Sammy, and me. I think that I should pay for this one because the room is certainly out of Gunvald's price range. He is in India for a long time and needs to watch his money. Edith asked me to take care of the room for Sammy and she will pay for his meals. Edith and I have agreed to split the cost of the taxi, which is fair. I recall her saying that Gunvald should not have to pay for the taxi because he is a student while I am a lawyer. European tax logic, that is okay.

Sammy, Gunvald and I settle into our large room. We are going to have a quick lunch here and then Sammy is going to take us on a short tour of a spice plantation.

We are driving through the hills in the calming countryside. Our windows are open letting the warm breeze blow against our faces and hair. Trees and brush line the dusty road. We pull up to a gate and a teenage boy shows Sammy where to park. We get out of the car and are greeted by two other boys. Often the tour guide is helpful. In particular when you do not have a clue where you are or what you are looking at. There are plenty of little Indian boy tour guides around. We get three and do not mind at all. Since Sammy stayed with the car, we have three guides for four tourists. Of course these young men expect to be paid and they should because they are not in your face. Our guides are energetic and polite. The youngest boy is eight years old and named Ravi. He eyes up my water bottle so I pull a bottle out of my pack and give it to him. Edith grins as I take his picture while walking backwards up the slope.

Ravi acts the role of botanist during our slow and deliberately walk up the sandy brown path toward the top of the mountain. Believe it or not, learning about all the different teas is interesting. This is a nice change of scenery, topography and elevation. The air becomes cooler as we walk higher.

There is a canopy of green everywhere. Tall trees, with thin branches, are spread out along the base of a mountain alongside tall green bushes and short stubby bushes. A few, not so alive, spindly trees stand, showing their loss of a long struggle with thicker vegetation over water. It is another example of new life replacing the old.

We do not suffer any adverse affects from the elevation. We breathe easy and do not sweat. The mountain slope is terraced. Every square foot of soil is utilized. The plants are all in unison; row and column. The tea plants are short and cute, just like our guides. I have always wondered what a tea plant looked like. They remind me of hilling potatoes with mom, in the garden next door at the old house. Tea plants are more feminine, with much smaller leaves than the rugged potato. We are told that there are many varieties of tea at this plantation. Most of the tea is exported. Our guides do not know how much of it is processed here.

The drive back to Periyar is relaxing after the refreshing walk up the mountain. A small hill compared to the Canadian Rocky Mountains but to many people here, it is indeed a mountain.

The dinner at the hotel is quite good. Edith and Harry say that they are going to take it easy tonight so Gunvald, Sammy and I leave them be and have a small quiet little party in our room. We have plenty of beer to drink and cricket to watch on television. Sammy sure likes his beer.

It is late morning and Sammy is driving us to the boat tour parking lot. The pamphlet for the tour states that tigers are in abundance here. I get excited, but realize that it is next to impossible to catch a glimpse of a tiger from a boat on a lake. Nevertheless, one has to be positive and keep a good lookout in order to prevent missing the slim chance. The wind off the water cools our skin. Harry puts on a Arab styled veil. It is deep black. The joker looks like a cross between a ninja and a man wearing a Burka. In fact, I think that it is a Burka. We see some wild boars grazing on patches of grass next to the lakeshore. That is the extent of the wildlife seen from the boat, except for birds and fish. That is okay.

We go out for a late lunch, which is good. Late lunches are relaxing, especially if you eat light, have water and stick to one beer.

Gunvald and I walk outside the restaurant and see a mature elephant. He is large, looks wise and strong. Looking into his eyes I smile and introduce myself as swami. I tell him that I think he is one of God's most beautiful creatures. His skin is course and covered with fine bristly hairs. He is gentle. His eyes are deep and full of wisdom. Eyes can be a window to the soul.

As I sit on the great beast's back the Mahout leads him. I love elephants as much as I love whales. I want to ensure that he receives a good supper tonight from his Mahout. Gunvald takes our picture and says, "swami, you and the elephant look good together."

"Thank you Gunvald. It would be a little more exciting if I had the express consent of this wonderful creature and we were walking along in a jungle, seeking out a vat of fermenting beer. I am sure that he would prefer that to walking up and down the same alleyway many times each day."

"Do you really think that elephants like beer swami?"

"Why wouldn't they? Unless they are a more mature elephant and have switched to vodka."

Madurai, what a city! It is so different and exciting with it's temples standing out majestically. I take a picture of Harry on his and Edith's balcony of their room, which is adjacent to Gunvald's, Sammy's and mine. You can tell that Harry is really fired up. We all are. I can sense why, the stay at Periyar was boring. Madurai is full of life and hustle and bustle. It is the second largest city in Tamil Nadu. Madras or Chennai is the largest in this state. I read, while doing some research on India before leaving Canada, that Madurai is one of the oldest cities in India, being over 2500 years old. We decide to hang around our hotel room, it is too late in the day to go out and tour. Gunvald and Sammy watch the girls dance on television while I read the India Times newspaper. I then spend a good hour on the balcony, looking at the surrounding buildings and the busy street below.

Across the street, from our balcony, I see a young Indian woman is hanging laundry on a line. Her family has a top floor apartment with a small deck. I watch her work for some time. She looks toward me a few times. She waves and I wave back. It is all good. I rejoin the boys inside. We take it easy on the beer, we have a big day of touring tomorrow and we will be starting early.

It is early morning. I walk out to the balcony to watch the rest of the sunrise. I see a young boy of about eleven years of age standing on the sidewalk across the street. He leans his back and head against a building's wall. His right foot is planted against the wall resulting in a cool posture. He looks up and waves. I point to my chest and then point to him.

On the sidewalk we exchange pleasantries. Silva is a twelve year old guide going on thirty-five. He has excellent manners, pretty damn good English and nice looks. He is a charming young man. I like the kid so much because his smile is vibrant and true. Silva has short dark curly hair, clean around the ears and an uneven bang over his eyebrows. He comes across as cunning and street smart.

Over breakfast, across the street from our hotel, Silva tells us that his mother is ill. He does not have a father and his younger sister is six years old. I do not judge him but Edith figures he is a street con. I think he is a professional tour guide for white people in Madurai. So what if he wants to be paid for being a very nice and charming guide. I think he will be a great guide and a gentleman.

The restaurant is cafeteria style, with the menus displayed on boards high on the wall. I order tea and toast along with Edith and Harry. Gunvald has the Thali meal. Silva has eaten breakfast so I offer to buy him a soda.

The Meenakshi Radharani temple is huge and intimidating to the wary. It can be seen in the far distance. The outside walls are adorned with thousands, if not millions, of Hindu deity carvings from the temple's foundation to its roof. There are two towering sanctuaries which Silva says are called gopurams. Madurai is an ancient city within a surrounding countryside, layered with coconut groves and vast rice fields. The grounds are filled with brightly dressed Hindu pilgrims, Indian tourists and a small percentage of foreign tourists.

We enter the temple and find that it is large and dark. Candles lay inset in the walls. Symbols clash loudly. The smell of incense permeates. Hindu deities are in abundance. The monks prance about proudly to the deep thumping sounds of beating drums. We come to a shrine enclosing a three-foot image of Shiva. Sunlight from a small wall opening, falls upon it. Harry dips his finger in the dry red powder and rubs some of it between his eyebrows. Gundvald and I do the same. When in a Hindu temple, act as a Hindu. We see many shrines honoring the major deities. A few of the deities are familiar, some I have not seen before.

We are walking to another shrine situated in a courtyard outside, when a young pilgrim man of twenty years sees me and stops me.

He says, "You Sir, you are special man. You are so big and big with life! I can see something almost Godlike in you." He then places a ten Rupee bill in my front shirt pocket.

"Thank you Sir but I do not deserve this." I state while returning the bill.

"You are such a strong and happy man full of spirit."

I say, "I truly thank you for saying that." He hugs me and leaves. I hope that I will meet him again, outside the walls of this crowded and busy temple. People here are very alive. It would have been nice to find out more about the young pilgrim's insight that seemed to come from within the heart. Maybe it is good luck for a Hindu to see a white man in the temple. I doubt it but what do I know about that?

Gundvald and I walk back inside the temple and decide to explore. Silva stays with us while Edith and Harry are content taking a seat on a stone ledge. You can feel the intensity in the air. The sounds are shrill, loud and forceful. I could spend hours here, walking through the hallways, inspecting every nook and carving and seeing all the rooms. This is not a museum with wide hallways and corridors. It is crowded. Pilgrims will spend days to travel to this place. I can see why. It is large and has many detailed deities to honor.

Silva says, "More than ten thousand people visit here every day and thirty thousand on a Friday because it is a special day for Meenakshi, the three breasted goddess." Silva blushes.

I laugh and say, "*TOO MUCH.*"

We walk over to Harry and Edith. I say, "Edith, it would be very cool to visit this temple at night."

"No thank you swami." says Edith.

"I will come with you at night swami." Harry states.

Edith asks, "Are you sure that you are strong enough my dear Harry?"

"Hey honey, I am a tough guy. I am strong."

I state, "Harry is a strong man Edith. I think I see what you are getting at. You think that we could get freaked out. The only thing that would freak me out is if someone pulls a knife on me."

"Yes swami. You and I could take on anyone or anything together."

Edith jokes, "You men think that you are so tough."

"Edith, to be a good content being a man requires a certain degree of strength. One must be strong mentally and physically in order to fly over the barriers presented to us in life. The same goes for women."

"Oh swami. Such a swami." Says Edith as she hugs me.

Harry speaks in a forced sad voice, "Don't get too touchy feely with swami Edith. You are my lady."

Edith and Gunvald continue to laugh when I say, *"DO NOT WORRY HARRY, SWAMI WOULD NOT EVEN THINK OF CUTTING YOUR FLOWERS OR MASSAGING YOUR LADY. YOU ARE THE MASSEUSE AROUND HERE BRO."*

It is late in the day and we are in a corridor of a temple that has many booths selling souvenirs. We leave and I carry two Shiva and Vishnu deities are under my left arm. *Always try to leave your stronger arm free kid. You never know when you might need it. Even in the most mellow or peaceful set-*

ting, your free strong arm may come in handy, especially if you trip often when on holiday.

Once Edith, Gunvald, Harry, Sammy and I group together outside the temple Silva excitingly states, "Mr. swami, let me take you to the finest rooftop restaurant in Madurai. It is seven stories up with a wonderful view. The food is excellent. I am sure you will enjoy it."

We drive past shoppers on Marret Street. Silva whispers in my ear, "Mr. swami, that young Hindu thought you were like a God."

"Mr. swami is no God Silva. Life is easy, just give as much love as you can with actions."

Sammy parks next to a hotel called the Classic Residency. It is in the heart of downtown Madurai and looks high end. Silva leads us into the hotel and toward the elevator. The doorman briefly stops Silva. Silva motions his hand toward our group and the doorman realizes that Silva is our guide and is taking us up for dinner.

Once outside on the roof I notice the manager look and smile at Silva. He must bring many tourists here. The manager approaches our table after we are seated. Silva looks so proud as he stands and introduces us to the manager. He should receive a good commission for taking us here. Good for Silva. We would not have found this place on our own. It has a very large terrace with fabulous views. There are red brick walls stopping at four feet so not to interfere with the wonderful view. The kitchen is in one corner enclosed by three walls, leaving the kitchen open to our view. There must be 2000 square feet of open area up here. It is a similar set up to Suki's rooftop restaurant. It is great being removed from the hustle and bustle of the markets.

The menu is diverse offering South Indian, North Indian, Chinese and continental cuisine. After discussion and consensus regarding our food order over drinks, (no I did not offer Silva any booze), Silva orders the meal. We decide on Chinese.

The food arrives and you can see the steam rise from the plates. It is well presented and looks appealing. It tastes very good. We eat slowly except for Sammy. He eats like someone is going to take his plate away. I thought that Gunvald ate fast. Edith, like most ladies, likes to dine and take her time.

A young woman named Anna, is sitting at the next table. She is a twenty-five year old nanny who has been three months in India. She is on her way to meet her new family in Madras. I am having such a great time with my friends that I do not flirt with her, despite that she subtly flirts with me. I listen to her story for ten minutes while we eat. I have too much experience, friendship and love for life going on to allow my sausage to get into the way of things. Even though I am the one talking to Anna, Gunvald has his eye on her. We are leaving in the morning and therefore there is insufficient time to get to know Anna. I am not into one night stands. A good man gets to know a woman well before he sleeps with her. *When you get older Keenan and become a good man, which could take you into your early thirties, you will not want to sleep with your lady friend until you love her deeply. Love your neighbor is not all-encompassing.* For those who don't get this, Jesus did not mean make love to all your attractive neighbors. He meant that you should love your fellow man.

I ask Silva to write down his name and address. He refuses looking embarrassed. It seems that he cannot. It hits me. The kid is street and tourist smart, yet he cannot write. I know that he can read small sentences because he pointed out signs, menu items and directions. Edith mentioned the possibility of Silva being illiterate earlier. I hoped that he had at least his grade three or equivalent and chose the path of the tourist guide to help his family. I want to help him and stay in contact. We chip in for dinner and Edith and I agree to Silva's tip. Silva counts his tip and gleams, eyes wide, like a poor boy getting a brand new bike on his twelfth birthday.

"You are a cool man swami." Silva says while we pause on the sidewalk outside of the hotel.

"You are a groovy young man Silva. Keep on smiling and being happy with yourself and what you do."

"Thank you swami, thank you everyone. I must go home now." Silva shakes hands with the others, gives me a hug and runs down the sidewalk toward home.

We wake up early and go for breakfast after checking out of our hotel. We will be going to our last destination, Kodaikanal, when we finish eating. It is 120 kilometers from Madurai. Edith says that it is a most beautiful hill resort and when walking on the side of a mountain, the clouds will be below our feet.

The drive up the steep road to Kodaikanal is arduous. The road winds and quickly narrows in spots. It is crazy when a bus passes us coming down the mountain road. There is no room for error. The bus slows to a stop while inching past us. There are many monkeys, hanging around in trees, on both sides of the road. You can tell that the monkeys are not nervous as they play about.

Half way up the mountain, we stop for some chi at a landing area beside a teashop. Edith, Gunvald and I have a cigarette. Harry does not usually smoke and Sammy does only when he has a few beers. Good for them. We look at the scenery but become more interested in a tour bus, slowly navigating a sharp turn, far up the road from us.

Edith says, "There is not much room for that bus to make the corner. Look, he has to back up."

Sammy announces, "Do not worry about bus driver. He does not want to die. He drives up this mountain for his living. Crazy road needs good patient driver."

We choose the Hotel Astoria, Kodaikanal. Sammy drives to it like he knew where he is going. The rooms are just over 300 rupees per night so we book in for two nights. As Gunvald, Sammy and I settle into our meager room I suggest, "Boys, shall I go get us some beer to relax with before we go explore the town?"

"Great idea swami. What do you think Sammy?" Gunvald says.

Sammy says, "Yes," and does the head wiggle.

I stop at the front desk and ask the clerk named Raj where I can buy beer for our room. He explains the address and I ask for him to draw me a map.

Raj says, "No. Mr. swami you do not need a map. Go outside, turn right and then walk for two minutes and look right. You will see a small shop of unpainted concrete with a few stairs going up. He is our neighbor." I thank Raj and wonder if Sammy knows that the liquor store is so close.

When I say store Keenan, you need to close your eyes and ignore any liquor store that you have ever been in. The shelves are made of wooden planks supported by stacked bricks. There are not any coolers. There is not even a cash register. I ask for twelve Kingfishers and the cashier pulls out a box that already has a dozen in it. I pay him and he gives me the change out of his pocket. I feel a beer bottle to see if it is warm and it is not. It is on the cooler side.

"If you want to keep them cool in your hotel room, put some in the toilet tank." the clerk states.

"Thank you Sir."

I open the door to our room and I find Gunvald and Sammy watching television. They are watching the music video channel from Bombay. "Hello swami, any trouble finding beer?" Gunvald asks.

"No buddy, it is around the corner. I think Sammy picked this hotel simply because of the beer store location. Would you believe that the beer is only thirty Rupees each and they are cool right off the shelf."

Sammy is all smiles. I open three beers, put three in the toilet tank and another three in the sink and fill it with cold water. We watch the girls dance and enjoy our cool beer. Perhaps being on the side of mountain equals cool beer. It even seems to taste better for the boys at thirty Rupees each. Sammy is starting to get a buzz on as he finishes his second beer. No problem, he does not have to drive today or early tomorrow. Sammy does not smoke pot because it makes him sleepy. Gunvald and I enjoy one and blow the smoke out the window.

"Sammy, it is a good thing not to smoke and get sleepy, you are professional driver." I say.

Sammy says, "Thank you for the beer swami."

"You are welcome Sammy. You are a good driver and you deserve a break. Today and tonight is the best time on the tour to drink good."

"For you and I also swami." Gunvald says. "We do not have a tour today and have the rest of the day to do what ever we like."

"Here's to the three of us, a great afternoon and a party tonight. Cheers boys!" I say.

Gunvald suggests, "Let's go buy another box of beer and walk around and explore the place."

"Sounds good to me Gunni." I reply.

We walk along the sidewalk while I stay back a few yards to see if Sammy knows where the store is. Sure as hell, he turns right and marches up the steps of the beer store. I pay, while Sammy pitches in a hundred Rupees. Gunvald and I are going to settle up on everything later. We take our beer and walk up the crested street. It is not that steep but I feel strain in my shins after a few blocks. We arrive at what seems like a small park and find a bench to rest on. Our surroundings are silent. There are not any stores on this end of the street. The sun peeks out at us through intermittent clouds.

Gunvald is a great guy who smokes beggar cigarettes. The poorest of the poor, who happen to smoke, enjoy what are called beedees. I am not sure of the spelling. They are rolled in a coarse tight leaf that resembles a thin cardboard. It is a leaf from the lowliest of tobacco plants. A beedee is about two inches long, tapered to a couple millimeters at the inhaling end and about a quarter inch at the other end. They taste like shit.

I open a beer using a lighter for Sammy. He is grinning so good, all I can think of is Sammy Davis Jr. on stage with Dean Martin and Frank Sinatra, having a party. I take a pack of Scissors Filters out of my fanny pack, open it and start to pull a cigarette out. Sammy grabs one and grins. I then put one in Gunvald's mouth and then my own and light them all. I stand up, step away, turn to face the boys and start a few lines from Dean Martin's best known song.

The boys laugh with beer and cigarettes waving. We are like a 'Rat Pack' right now.

Gunvald asks, "You were not singing to us I hope."

"Gunvald, swami is not gay." Sammy snickers.

"Gunvald, it was us three singing to the women of the world but you two do not know the words of the song otherwise you would have joined in after the first line. Therefore I had to continue for us without you."

He replies, "Go on then, smart lawyer swami. Sing the next verse but do not look at us. Look at the sky please."

The sun has almost set and we are walking down a darkened street. We approach the light of a late night food stand. The stand is painted white and brightly lit. The menu is displayed on the back wall in English with big letters in black paint. Gunvald, Sammy and I are drinking beer on the side of the road; smoking cigarettes and marveling at the Indians in winter coats walking in various directions.

A man comes out from the back of his store. He looks a lot different than the locals. He has an oval face topped with a brimless small black hat. Some people call them 'Tope' hats. It is cool looking, with a flat round top and five inch cylindrical side. He wears a white shirt with a black vest. No parka. His skin is fair and has an olive tone to it. He is tall, thin and stoic. He reminds me of Swami Vivekananda. In good English without an Indian accent he asks us, "Are you men hungry for some good food? I also make Western food."

"Perhaps." I reply. "What Western food can you cook?"

"The best hamburger in all of India." He says with a coy smile. I am on to him.

"*HOW THE HELL ARE YOU GOING TO MAKE US A HAM-BURGER? YOU NEED A COW FOR BURGER. YOU SHOULD GO TO THE TEMPLE AND SAY YOUR PRAYERS.*"

He is laughing good. "What is your name Sir?"

"*I AM SWAMI WITH A SMALL 's'. THE PALE GUY IS GUNVALD. HE IS FROM NORWAY AND IS THE GRANDSON OF A GREAT WHALESMAN. THIS SHORT AND GOOD LOOKING INDIAN IS SAMMY. HE IS NAMED AFTER A FAMOUS SINGER AND COME-DIAN, SAMMY DAVIS JUNIOR.*"

"That is a pretty good Indian accent. I know who Sammy Davis Junior is and you are right. Your Sammy could be the son of Davis Junior. Now, how the hell did you get the name swami? That is an Indian name. You are not an Indian, not even close. You are from across the ocean and you sound Canadian."

Gunvald and Sammy are getting a kick out of this guy; obviously so am I.

"Yes I am Canadian. How did you guess, eh? I got the nickname from a young man from Bombay named Sonny. We were in Kanyakumari, after meeting on the train, walking by a statue of Swami Vivekananda. As we walk by, Sonny stops and looks up at the statue's face. He then looks at me in the eyes and says, 'Mr. Brent, you are a swami. I am going to call you swami'. The name stuck and now that I have a broader understanding of the meaning of the word 'swami', I am proud to have it. What is your name and where did you learn English so well?" I open a beer and hand it to him.

"My name is Tariq. I am originally from Northern Pakistan. My English is good because I went to University in England. I have spent time in the United States but I have not been to Canada."

Gunvald asks, "Tariq, how did you end up on the top of a mountain selling food?"

"I came here when I was a child and have many fond memories here. The clouds below you, the coolness of the air make this place so damn unique. To me it is like heaven. A lot of money comes through this mountain. Many wealthy Indian tourists come here. After I completed my education and traveling I set up a business in Pakistan and did okay. Years later, I was not fully happy, neither was my family. I did not like Pakistan either. You did not know when you could get shot or shaken down. You had to hide your wealth and make sure you did not look too big or successful. The Muslim clerics were getting too greedy and powerful. You are not free in Pakistan. I am free on this mountain."

"That is fantastic. Good on you man." I say.

Tariq asks us, "How are you finding India?"

"Go ahead Gunvald. I am going to grab a round of beers out of the box." I hand one to Sammy and say, "Now Sammy, don't be getting too drunk again. You are not a good driver when you are hung over, half-pissed and show blood shot eyes." Sammy pats me on the shoulder and exudes his big Sammy Davis smile, showing his big pearly white teeth.

I hand Gunvald and Tariq a beer.

Gunvald says, "India is cool and spiritual. It is rich in history and people. I like the warmth and the prices. This cool mountain air is very refreshing."

"Thanks for the cigarette swami, now give me a light." Tariq sarcastically says. Gunvald gives me a look so I hand him a cigarette after lighting Tariq's.

This fella is really cool. Tariq has been around. He has had big business in Delhi and Bombay after Pakistan. He says, "I got tired of the stress of big business and scaled down. So here I am, out of the heat and away from the increasingly commercialization of life. This mountain is my modern Eden."

"What about you swami, is India treating you well?"

"Tariq, this swami is having the most spiritual and learning experience in my life. India is magical. It has allowed me to get all the negative shit out of my head and soul and be one with nature and our Creator God. I have felt our Creator's energy and my recently deceased father's soul, impact my body less than a week ago. Being negative free is the only way to be."

Tariq replies, "That is interesting swami. I would like to talk to you more about your spiritual awakening. I do not open for lunch until eleven in the morning. Tomorrow I am coming in around at about 8:00 a.m.. Please come by if you can."

"I will Tariq. Fellas, swami needs to take a leak."

Gunvald says, "Me too."

Sammy adds, "Let us piss in the ditch like drunken Indians."

"Please excuse us Tariq, we will be right back."

"All right swami," Tariq replies and chuckles.

We line up, laugh and shake the dew off the lily.

"Do you think Mr. Burger Man Tariq will actually make us hamburgers?" I ask.

"There is no hamburger in all of India. Maybe a McDonalds in Bombay though." Answers Sammy. "Maybe it will be minced goat."

Gunvald pipes, "As long as it tastes good, looks good and does not make me sick I will be happy."

"Well, let's shake off and go find out. Don't drip on your hands because there are not any washrooms in sight boys." We laugh. Not because it was that funny just because we have had a few. The cheap beer is cooler along with the late evening mountain air.

We return to Tariq's stand. "Mr. swami. They are almost ready, the best burgers in India, coming right up."

Tariq delivers our burgers and yes, no hamburger is to be found. The meat has more of a ham taste than ground beef. The sauce over the imposter burger is good, not too sweet and a little spicey. We thank Tariq and finish our beer. Back at the hotel room, we drink more beer and watch the girls dance on the Delhi music channel. I write notes in time to the girls moving their hips. We stay up very late and have a good party.

I wake up early. The sun is not quite up. There is not an ocean to swim in so perhaps a walk and stop over at Tariq's will be eventful. After leaving a note for Gunvald and Sammy I walk out and decide to start out down-hill and stop by Tariq's stand on the way back.

An hour passes in quiet retrospection and peacefulness.

The swinging horizontal door of Tariq's newly dubbed Burger Emporium, is not open so I knock on it. Silence. Thirty seconds elapse. I knock again and put my ear to the door. Nothing. A tap on my left shoulder suddenly startles me. I jump and hit my head on the door jam.

"Sorry to startle you swami but I could not resist. Are you bleeding?"

I take off my hat and feel the side of my head. "None felt you bugger."

"Well, good morning to you then. Let's go for some chi and a short walk."

"Chi will hit the spot, along with some water."

We walk away with Tariq leading. I ask him, "Please tell me about your God Tariq."

"I am not a unmoving Darwinist nor am I an unbending Creationist. Perhaps the truth contains aspects of both theories. What I do know is that the universe is energy; humans and life consist of energy."

"I agree with you. I am not ready to write religion off due to the Abraham stories."

"Why do you think the Abraham story is important?" asks Tariq.

"Well, I find it fascinating that the three world religions, Judaism, Christianity and Islam, have attempted to claim the story of Abraham as their own. There has to be some historical truth about Abraham. I think that the Abraham story has had much impact on the Jewish-Palestinian conflict in the holy land. Since a teenager I have been trying to figure out the root of the intense hatred between the followers of Islam and Judaism—Isaac and Ismail. This hatred, coupled with America's support of Israel, is the root of what makes the world so unstable today."

"You will not find the answers to life with religion alone. I am sure that you are well aware that religions make the world unstable. Jesus preached against religion. In fact, the staunch following of religion prevents you from obtaining a more comprehensive and objective understanding of life. We will have to leave the remainder of our discussion for mail, swami."

"I agree with you on both counts Tariq. One needs only faith and the rest will come later. We could talk about this for months. Please tell me more about you, your family and your business."

He does and finishes by saying, "That's enough about me. Now let me tell you my favorite lawyer joke before we part. After you get married some day bring your wife to this beautiful place."

"I sure will. Tell me your joke please." I reply.

"A Mafia Godfather discovers that his accountant has cheated him out of thirteen million dollars. The accountant is deaf and that is the reason he was hired in the first place. It was assumed that a deaf accountant would not hear anything that he might have to testify about in court. When the Godfather goes to confront the accountant about the missing thirteen million, he brings his lawyer, who knows sign language. The Godfather advises the lawyer, 'Ask him where the thirteen million he stole from me.' The lawyer asks the accountant, in sign language, where the stolen money is."

"The accountant signs back, 'I do not know what the hell you are talking about. The lawyer tells the Godfather, 'He says that he doesn't know what you are talking about."

"The Godfather pulls out a handgun, presses it against the accountant's temple, and says, 'Ask him again.' The lawyer signs to the accountant, 'He will kill you if you don't tell him!'"

I am liking the joke so far while Tariq is smiling knowing that I will not take offence.

"The accountant signs back, 'OK! You got me. The money is in a brown briefcase, buried behind the shed in my nephew Leo's backyard in Queens!' The Godfather asks the lawyer, 'Well, what did he say?'"

The lawyer replies, "'He says that you don't have the balls to pull the trigger.'"

Sammy is ready for breakfast. Gunvald is in the shower. There is a knock at the door. It is Harry. "We are ready to go down for breakfast. We will meet you in the restaurant in ten minutes. What the hell did you guys do in here last night? It smells like stale beer and cigarettes. Sammy, your eyes are bloodshot. You should open a window."

"Relax Harry. It is obvious that you did not get much beer last night. Sammy is alright. After some breakfast and coffee he will be fine to drive in an hour." I respond. "We are not traveling on the highway. I will drive if need be."

Harry replies, "Are you being funny swami? You may not have blood shot eyes but can you drive here?"

"If I must and everyone in the cab is quiet, except for Edith the navigator."

Edith, Harry, Gunvald, Sammy and I now stand on a hill overlooking part of the town and it's lake. Kodaikanal is beautiful. It is amongst the Palani Hills, which are essentially foothills of the Western Ghat Mountains. The main attraction here is Lake Kodaikanal, which lays still below us within a plateau, enclosed by moderately sloped and subtle wooded hills.

Keenan, just because you are enjoying the beauty of today does not mean that you must have the same experience of beauty tomorrow. Today matters, tomorrow is after you wake up after falling asleep following a good time.

I point over to the Perumal Malai Mountain. It is larger than a hill and about half the size of Mount Keenan. *Remember the mountain outside Jasper, one of the first large ones you see with a vertical face ending in a flat top, that I named after you Keenan.* It is quiet here with no wind. Despite being a holiday resort, Kodaikanal is not full of tourists, the resort is spread out wide, high and low. We saw a large tourist bus depot last night and there were more than ten buses parked there. This is better than Banff in some ways. The mountains and companion hills are soft and feminine. The hills remind me of a certain nurse I worked with years ago. The hourglass figure in a white nurse's uniform, outlining where her thighs met her hips, then contouring up to her thin waist. The line goes up and her modest bosom and shoulders finish off her lovely figure with strength and curvaceous beauty. Oh yeah, she was also smart and caring. The human mind prefers roundness and curves over sharp edges. That is why the rolling hills of the Qu' Appelle Valley kick butt over the rough peaks of the Rocky Mountains.

We are slow-stepping along Coaker's Walk, which is cut into the hillside. We stop and look down to the plain below. The cloud is becoming denser and is rising slowly up to us. We stand in silent awe. We are entranced with nature's gifts standing out before us. It is an excellent vantage point.

The cloud is one dense mass of fog, layered and flat. At this moment, it lays twenty-five feet or so below us. It is unlike flying in an airplane at 35,000 feet, we are not removed from the pillow like mattress of a cloud. I get the feeling that I can jump down on it and bounce back to where we stand. It is a sifting loose fog cloud, slowly rising and expanding within the valley. One cannot help but feel that you are within a handshake of our Creator. We stand in silence, watching, mesmerized.

Sammy is driving us to a very large hotel on the lake. It is called 'The Carlton' which is a big British name and appropriate since it is a five star ritzy place. By the way, I noticed a rudimentary golf course coming into the resort. A golf course on a mountain plateau in India? It is quite unexpected, despite that Kodaikanal is a big tourist destination for wealthy Indian tourists. Edith wants to go in to the Carlton, even if she has to pay 150 rupees for a tea! Figure that. A tight ass German paying five bucks for a cup of tea. Who's the fool? I am. Edith ends up paying thirty rupees for a coffee and biscuit, Gunvald pays forty rupees for a cold coffee, which goes good with his beggar cigarettes, he says. I pay almost one hundred rupees for a beer. I buy Sammy and I one each.

The scenery surrounding our table is unbelievably immaculate and serene. The manicured grass, people paddling on the calm lake with an abundance of colorful flowerbeds and birdbaths, instill the desire to sit back in your chair and peacefully ponder. Two birds land in a ceramic birdbath and splash about. Three more flutter around a bird feeder under a tree. Two birds are dancing on the ground beneath a birdbath, in the sunlight, shaking their feathers, ridding the wetness so it is no longer there.

Gunvald and I are walking along a path, with Edith and Harry sauntering behind, while Sammy is with the car. We are on a portion of the mountain valley that has a large plateau, not far from the lake. There are Catholic and Hindu shrines situated around the park. Interestingly, there are a few small English style cottages in the center of the grounds. Gunvald and I sit on some grass analyzing a Catholic shrine that contains some of the stations of Jesus being abused. We get up, without saying anything, and walk down the small slope. Gunvald looks toward one of the cottages and excuses himself from my company. Gunvald is checking out one of the cottages and looks in the windows. It is a small cottage and it does not take him long to circle and inspect it. An old Indian woman approaches Gunvald from another cottage that is a twin to the one that Gunvald is interested in. He talks to her and then approaches Sammy and I, beside the car. This is it. I know it Goodbye to my new brother.

"My dear friend swami, I am going to stay at that cottage for awhile."

"Gunvald, this is a surprise."

"Well swami, you must have known that I would not be going back to Kovalam. I must move on and travel."

"That is true my friend. This is an excellent place to stay for a few days. Why move back when you should and are able to move forward."

"Yes swami. You have been a fun, generous and good friend. You take care of yourself and write the book. Let's settle up with what I owe you."

Just like that, a hug later and he is gone. Wow! I have grown attached to him. It is good to have a friend by your side. I will see him again, that is for sure. He will have a swell time in this fabulous little Eden.

We are driving back to Kovalum Beach, Edith is playing with the radio when she says, "In Germany, the government taxes its citizens on their car radios and the televisions in their homes. Europeans are taxed very heavily." I think the reason is because Europeans may be more altruistic than Westerners. I do not get into it, it is morning and not a time for political debate, after cocktail hour is, unless you are a square politician.

Sammy is navigating a two-lane highway, which has no centerline or shoulders, when we see a gravel truck laying in the ditch on its side. A few minutes later we see a flat bed truck also on its side. Edith says that she has counted five so far.

"They think they own the road," pouts Edith. She appears to be suffering from a hangover and is somewhat bitchy this morning. She is also concerned over her relationship with Harry. She is right. A big truck will not let us pass. Sammy sees an opening and starts to pass. There is very little room. The truck does not pull over to the right at all.

I yell out to the truck driver as we pass, "Editha marthira mayday!" Do not ask me what this actually means. Harry and the Sammy taught me this earlier. They say it means something like, 'go to hell you asshole'. I do not believe them because these two Indians like to bullshit.

Sammy steers his taxi into the parking lot of the train station in Trivandrum. The ticket manager says that the train going to Madras is booked for the next week. *WHAT THE HELL DEAR LADY. THIS WHITE SWAMI NEEDS TO GET TO MADRAS IN TWO DAYS TO CATCH*

HIS FLIGHT BACK HOME TO CANADA. I DO NOT MIND TO RIDE IN THE BACK CAR WITH WOODEN SEATS SITTING AMONGST THE POOR. PLEASE FIND ME A SEAT MADAM FOR NEXT DAY."

She grins and says, "I will put you on a waiting list. You will be sixteenth on the list but if there are some cancellations you may get a ticket. Show up tomorrow morning to see if you are fortunate."

"Thank you very much." I walk to the cab somewhat anxious about obtaining a seat on the train. I have to be across the country in Madras in a few days for my flight while the trip takes about twenty-four hours. There are two days to spare but I really want that morning train. There must be a certain amount of seats for foreign tourists. The situation reminds me of my best buddy Lou's father's not so famous but should be famous line, "Don't piss before your water comes."

Edith asks me, "Did you get your ticket swami?"

"No, Edith. The clerk put me on a waiting list. I am hopeful." I imagine sitting in the back booth of a train car, beside a pretty hippy, tree-hugging lady with a cute European accent.

The good news is that I am able to get my old room at Kovalam Beach for one more night.

After dinner, Harry, Edith and I saunter down the beach to My Dream. I see Paul and he waves.

"Hello Paul, how are things?" I ask.

Paul fills us in regarding Bernie following Minna to her first stop on her and Katarina's tour for a couple of days. It is not quite the same without Gunvald. I miss that bugger. Paul and the three of us talk and drink until we are cut off around 2:00 a.m., probably a good thing. Manager is happy to see me. I sure like that son-of-a-gun, he is a good man and a good host.

The early morning air pleasantly blows through Sammy's taxi windows. Edith and Harry discuss visiting Harry's sister in Trivandrum. Sammy patiently drives along the paved double-lane road, I think of making the train. There will be a seat for the swami; I know it.

Harry and Edith are sitting in the waiting area. I run up to them and show them my train ticket.

"That is great swami," says Harry, "I knew you would make the train. They save room for you white people and will also kick off a few Indians to make room for a foreign tourist."

"Good luck swami. Harry and I are going to miss you. Do not forget to write us. I want to know in advance when your book is coming out. I want you to bring a signed copy with you to India after it is complete." She hugs me firmly and kisses me on the cheek.

I reach out and shake Harry's hand. "You have been a fun friend Harry. Take care of yourself and continue to be a good man for Edith."

"Yes swami, I will. Enjoy the rest of your trip and watch out for those evil women."

"I sure will Harry. I thank you both for your company. You have really helped make my holiday and wake such a success, especially you Edith, for introducing me to Harry and Gunvald. Take care my friends."

"We thank you swami for your wonderful company. You are our swami. Goodbye." Edith states and gives me another hug.

I shake hands with Sammy, pick up my suitcase, and board the train.

The train is traveling North to Cochin and then East, across the country, to Madras. I plan to meet the Finnish ladies at a beach called Mahabalipuram, which is about forty kilometers South of Madras.

Three female European tourists are sitting in the three-sided cubicle with me. A young British lady is sitting to my left, looking out the window at the passing trees. After introductions, Karen whispers to me a story of her wet knickers. "I took five pairs of knickers to Zimbabwe. I brought ten pairs to India. When you hand wash them day after day the elastics wear out," she says with a subtle smile. (Hmm. I am correct in my thinking?). "They do fall down when they are wet", she adds. She is librarian cute with a touch of sexiness. I think she wants my sausage. That does not really matter for I am happy to sit next to her and listen. It is enjoyable to listen to Karen tell some of her life story. Time passes quickly.

The train is going to stop in Cochin shortly. We have been reading. "Karen, I am supposed to meet Kavi's Uncle in order to pick up my second suitcase. Keep mind of my things please."

"Sure swami."

The stop in Cochin turns out to be eventful and uneventful. I cannot see Mamea after standing for ten minutes at the doorway of our car. I decide to run down the platform and phone his house. There is no answer on the telephone after six rings, I hear from a distance a locomotive engine revving up and wheels squeaking. Holy lick! My train is leaving. I am running as fast as I can, racing up the concrete platform, chasing the train hard. Cigarette container flies out and so do the joints. I stop to pick them up and glance up. There is an army officer standing in the entrance area of a car. He does not pay attention to what I am picking up. I run my ass off to the car ahead of him, jump up and grab the side bar. The train is rolling faster and I miss my footing, my hip slams against the side of the railcar. I pull myself up and walk into the back of the car.

Shit, another army officer. I stand behind him. There are a good number of people standing about stretching their legs. Realizing that I do not belong in this car, drives me to act inconspicuously. "Do you have a seat Sir?" asks the soldier.

"*YES SIR, IN A CAR ABOUT FIVE CARS UP. I ALMOST MISSED THE TRAIN DURING THE STOP IN COCHIN TO PICK UP A BOX.*" I advise him that my ticket is with my luggage. It puts the minor matter to rest. Thank God that I have picked up the accent and am at ease and truly feeling swami. I should also thank Harry and Sammy as they also gave me a few lessons in rhythm and pitch.

"I will let you know of the next stop in advance. Then you can go to your seat. Do you remember the car number where you are seated?" The soldier asks sternly.

"*YES. THANK YOU SIR.*" I wiggle and stretch my head upwards and slightly sideways. He smiles back knowing that I have had much practice in saying yes with my square head.

After two quick stops, I manage to get back to my seat. Karen is relived to see me while the other two seat mates are surprised to see my return. I advise them of how lucky I am to convince the soldier that my ticket was here, and that I almost missed the train in Cochin.

The conversation with Karen continues. "In New Delhi the men were so rude, I had my bum fondled as I was walking down the sidewalk. It is crowded on the walks in the markets, and everywhere."

I ask Karen a couple of pertinent questions.

"No swami, I was with a man. Some of those guys are so bad. They think white tourists are loose because of western Hollywood stereotypes. I am from Europe. We try to respect fellow man and not be culturally insensitive. We stand up for ourselves and do not let the media control us.

We agree that it is silly to paint distinguishable people with the same brush. Even though most men across cultures are horn dogs, there are gentlemen among them. However, some cultures tend to walk on women.

A family sitting across the aisle from us begin to settle down for the night. It is amusing to witness the ingenuity of the beds being lowered and fixed into place. Karen is tired and also wants to sleep. She wants to sleep on top. I prefer the woman to be on top so she can take her pleasure. I help Karen lower her bed and excuse myself so she can ready herself for bed.

Bottle of water in hand, I sit down and let my legs hang out of the car opening. *Did I tell you Keenan, about the area at the end of most cars? A doorway lets you out of the car. The door closes with a knob and latch yet there is a one-inch space between the floor and the bottom of the door. Light can be seen between the top of the door and doorframe. There is a standing area about four feet deep and the width of the car, which must be at least thirteen feet wide. Looking outside there is no actual door, but an opening about five feet wide.*

While sitting comfortably I look at the stars. The stars do not pass as quickly like the landscape. It is a tranquil scene. Thanking God for the opportunity of being alive and able to be here just now. I light up a reefer, take three quick puffs, put it out and follow with a cigarette. No use taking chances on the Indian tobacco's pungent odor, wafting through the closed door of the train car.

The sound of the train rolling along the tracks is calming. Even the odd clank and twist rumbling is peaceful. There are no other sounds except the wind and train. The breeze is pleasant while the stars shimmer. Gunvald may be missed yet the stories of Charlie, body surfing, the wake and engagement party will not be forgotten. I take out my notepad and write about today and some thoughts for my good son.

Keenan, if in a conflict always use restraint and be polite. If a drunk wants to fight you, laugh, turn your back on him, walk briskly for three steps and turn around quickly. Now that you are out of reach you can size him up. Is he mad at you, the world or an ex-girlfriend? I have found that the phrase, 'What is troubling you brother?' often works. A handful of guys have bought me drinks for saying that. A few others have told me to fuck off. I ignored two of those except for one guy. He said something insulting about my mother. I really gave it to him hard but stopped once he hit the bar floor. Never punch or kick a man on the ground unless you and your country are at war with him. My advice for you and anyone else of a thinking mind, is that you do not fight any-one in school, on the street or in a bar. Too many cowards carry knives. Real men do not need to carry blades. Fools, gangsters and weak little evil bastards carry guns, in feeble attempts of protecting their little man complexes.

Nowadays, you fight one man you end up fighting a dozen and you will take a knife or a bullet. What happened to the good old days when a fistfight settled matters? Trouble is kid, those times only existed by chance. From day one, there has always been some little fucker ready to stab someone in the back. Keenan, it takes a bigger man to walk away from a fight. You should heed this advice because of the prevalence of guns and knives in schools.

On a lighter side son, try to face the little roadblocks in life as challenges. Some tests of determination can be quite rewarding. Some challenges do not require any determination, just some imagination. Let me tell you a story, but not in the past tense. That drives me nuts. I was walking down Clarence Ave-nue in Saskatoon, Saskatchewan one warm June afternoon. Nancy, my great friend from nursing college is walking beside me. There is a nice looking woman standing over her MG with the hood open. I say to the upset lady, "Excuse me Miss, can we help you?"

She answers yes and introduces herself as Lori, "The motor will not turn over."

I ask Lori, "Why don't you get in and try to start the motor so we can listen?" She does and turns the key. There is not the 'click click' sound of power not making it to the starter. Keep in mind Keenan, this is during the good old days when you could repair your own car because it had a carburetor and rotor, not a freaking computer. Power is present in the battery but it does not pass through the rotor.

I say, "There is power but it is not reaching the spark plugs and firing." Lori comes back to the motor and we pause for a moment. I then take off the top of the rotor cup that covers the spark plugs. I wiggle the spark plugs, one by one, and find the culprit. It is loose and the cap is moved aside. Without saying anything, I slowly take out a stick of Big Red bubble gum from my pocket, put it in my mouth and keep the rapper. Nancy and Lori look at me so I give them a stick each.

I fold the rapper, with the shiny side out, into a quarter-inch strip, wrap it around the top of the spark plug tip and snap the spark plug wire rubber connecter cap or boot back on.

"Try it now." I suggest. Lori returns to the car, turns the key and smiles big time to the sound of the motor. I get a good hug from Lori and her business card. You have to like those hugs when a lady pulls you in and presses her bosom against your chest.

Karen and I walk off the train, which is right on schedule. It is eight in the morning. It has been a twenty-one hour train ride including needed stops.

Karen and I share a man-peddled rickshaw to the bus depot. It not a pleasant experience as the driver is old and tired. He reminds me of the aged Cuban Santiago in Hemmingway's, *Old Man and the Sea.* I wish this guy drove an auto-rickshaw like I wished poor old Santiago steered a powerboat.

Back Together with the Finnish Ladies

Our bus arrives in Mamallapuram, Tamil Nadu, around 10:00 a.m.. It is a short taxi to Minna and Katarina's hotel. The rooms are all booked and I am advised that Minna and Katarina are at another beach.

The steps up to the roof of the restaurant are steep, sharp and could be threatening. I am following one of the hotel employees. I ask him, "Do you know which room the Finnish ladies are staying in? I am a friend of theirs and came here to meet them."

"On the main level, two rooms from the entrance."

"Thank you."

The clerk states, "We have mattresses for rent and you can sleep on the roof. We call this place the galaxy room." I look around and doubt that it would work. I would end up sleeping with one eye open.

"Thank you Sir, I may sleep on my girlfriends' floor."

Another fellow offers a fish, "Dear Sir. I am not into fish. I will not take your offer of an old fish that will sit around all day in the heat, while waiting for evening coals. I will drink your beer later."

I arrange for storage of my suitcase and set out to the ocean.

One cannot blame Minna and Katarina for going to a different beach. The beachfront here is riddled with poop and fisherman. One could handle the fisherman no doubt, but to have to navigate the boats, lines and crap is bothersome. The ocean is cool, while the waves are small and infrequent.

I am sitting at the restaurant overlooking the courtyard and the girls' room reading. Yes, for one of the few times in India, I am bored. I am not restless and the note writing is current. There is no problem being here; I must be around Madras for the flight home. The galaxy room may do, if I could lock up my belongings somewhere like Minna & Katarina's room. Hell, maybe I'll just sleep with them. The floor of their room will be suggested as we are friends and swami is not a pig.

I walk down the stairs and across the concrete courtyard to the door of Minna's and Katarina's room and place a note on their door, advising them that I am here and waiting on the roof top. *Keenan, do you ever notice that we mention the name of a person first and not second because the first seems to wear the pants in the relationship. I just realized that I mention Minna's name first as she is a little bossy over Katarina.* Anyway I leave the note, look at the simple concrete courtyard and walk up to the patio and order a beer.

The staffers here, albeit novice, assume that they can piss around with me. My server's name is Savat. He is almost trying to bully me into buying a fish. It is difficult to stop the con without the con's language and lingo. So once again I give it a go, *"WHAT THE HELL ARE YOU DOING? I AM NOT GREEN IN INDIA. YOU KNOW THAT WE SHOULD NOT EAT FISH THAT HAS SUNBATHED ALL DAY. GO TO THE TEMPLE AND SAY YOUR PRAYERS. DO NOT TRY TO FOOL THE SWAMI."* A surprised look results, but he understands the humor. I tip him a couple of American bucks with the beer order. He will not push the fish on me again.

The sun is very warm now. It peaks through the trellis and heats my skin. The beer cools the body and it is easy to drift away. I think of Edith and Harry. I miss them and Gunvald as well. It would be nice to see them again. I know why I am feeling a shade of melancholy. The trip will be over soon and I am waiting for the ladies. Waiting for them means missing them. Missing them means missing the others in the group. Damn it swami, it is far too early to miss anyone right now, so I concentrate on reading and note takings. How will I please my brain next? I say, give it some Gandhi. Man, I have even started to think words in my head like an Indian, let alone talk like one. *WHAT THE HELL KID, IT'S GONNA BE A BRIGHT, BRIGHT SUN SHINY DAY.*

The Hindus teach that there is great spiritual value in self-suffering. The Christians preach it but some rarely practice it. Gandhi took a crack at using spiritual laws in an attempt to overcome the all too often hatred between the Hindus and Muslims. A nation at war with itself is easily conquered.

Keenan, focus on qualities such as integrity, unconquerable courage, blunt truthfulness, love, wholeness and challenging evil. Never fear anyone or anything. It is okay to become scared on occasion. Your brain may be telling you to take care, be aware and protect your body. If you can harness life's energy and use it in a positive manner, nothing can stop you. Son, stand on your courage, convictions and the strength of your inner being and you will have great influence to help others and God. Yes my son, I have the balls to say that, I can and have, helped God. By simply helping others and serving God. Who is God? Really, God is the living energy that exists throughout the universe. Mother Nature, Love, reason for existence. Getting tingles up your spine while watching a duck and her ducklings waddle from one pond to another—even though you double bogeyed the last par five. Feeling so alive at sunrise and sunset. God is around us and within us. God is in you and around you. God is not just some conception in the sky or heaven pulling strings. God is Love and to understand Love is to be divine.

Evilness is the driving force behind those who promote non-existence, for example, radical Muslim leaders who conduct genocide in North Africa. Anyone who lacks a conscience for humanity is evil. You do not have to worship Satan to be evil. Many people who are evil, do not believe Satan or any supernatural entity exists. They exist for themselves for a short while and it is all over. Satan wants no worship; he does not simply exist as a sole physical entity but as very bad energy. Bad energy and evilness thrives from selfishness, cruelty and non-love in the world. Bad versus good. Evilness may take on the form of a physical entity, in one's own mind, in order for our under-used little brains to comprehend those who are evil and evilness in general.

The rich who want more and more, without giving a care about others, are not evil per se, hypocritical maybe. While not exactly evil, it is a sad fact that many in the West have turned their back on God and Love and embrace a commercialized life. I need a ninety thousand dollar car, a ten million dollar house and designer clothes for my kids in order to feel that I have done well for myself. This is what helps fuel the Muslim fire against the West.

Thank goodness Minna and Katarina show up so I can divorce myself from my philosophical rambling.

"Minna! Katarina!" I call out. They turn their heads and look up and wave. Then Minna makes a motion for me to come down. I move down the stairs quickly. "It is so nice to see you ladies again."

"You also swami." Minna chirps.

Katarina says, "It is mind bending to see you here on the other side of India. It is like time has not elapsed since Kovalam Beach."

Minna adds, "That is right Katarina. I feel it too. Were you able to get a room swami or would you like to stay with us?"

"Well thank you Minna. The rooms are all booked except the Galaxy room."

Katarina states, "You cannot sleep on the roof swami. It is not safe. Stay with us please."

"Thank you ladies very much. Your offer is accepted. Minna, don't you go making a move on me. You are an engaged woman."

"Oh swami. I have been satisfied funny man." She replies.

"What about me swami. Are you worried about Katarina making a move?"

"Katarina can take her pleasure with swami any time she wants."

"Hee hee hee." giggle Katarina and Minna.

"Paul told me about Bernie following you from Kovalam Minna. Was it romantic?"

"Very romantic. Surprisingly romantic." She answers.

"He loves you very much. He is a good funny man."

"He is. So swami, what would you like to do?" asks Minna.

"We could go shopping and for a drink." adds Katarina.

"That sounds great. Maybe we could go for a drink, shop, and then go for drinks."

We have a few beers at a restaurant not far from the hotel. Minna leads the way, through the small town, to the artesian tents. The scene is remarkable. Seeing these men, young and old, working away with chisels and sand paper on hard granite. I see a man about twenty-nine years old, bent over a table polishing a medium sized stone. He notices me looking at his displayed works spread over two long tables. He smiles when he sees my inquisitive eyes locked on a round, carved, granite stone, which is the size of a ladies fist. The color of the stone is a green-grey and its shape is perfectly round being roughly five inches in diameter. The Hindu symbol is there. Wow! I cannot believe it! Kukulkan is etched on the stone. He is the man with the beard who is responsible for teaching the Mayans to build their pyramids. He has helped more than one ancient culture construct pyramids and like structures of such magnificent design. *Keenan, for further information on this, read Graham Hancock.* The rock also has a marijuana leaf on it close to the man in the moon. A cross and the Ying Yang symbols are there too. Obviously, I buy it and do not bargain. Six hundred rupees. The receipt reads, One holy ball. On green stone—600 Rs./Queen Art Emporium. Specialists in Stone, Wood & Metal Carvings.

Following Katarina and Minna for the next half-hour is timeless. They are both so very pretty. It is quite relaxing just being a friend. Being a protector brother friend is also on the mind. We walk throughout the market, settling on the outside patio of a restaurant recommended earlier to Minna. Apparently she met the assistant manager a day earlier. We finish dinner and are sipping our wine when the supposedly assistant manager, named Katannal arrives at our table with a friend and sits with us. His friends name is Cheera. I do not like either of them; they come across as dishonorable knaves.

The bar service is closing early. It is not even 10:00 p.m.. Katannal suggests that we take his motorcycle and Cheera's scooter to another bar that he thinks will be open. I do not feel good about going somewhere with these guys but go along with it. I am sure as hell not going to let Minna and Katarina go alone with these good Karma resistant horn dogs. Indian women do not have sex before marriage. That fact tends to make Indian men all the more horny. Good for the women but the men seem to have trouble with that program. Minna and Katarina ride with Katannal and I with Cheera. After ten minutes of driving through town, including some dark streets to the edge of town, we arrive at a restaurant bar. It is dark. We walk to the entrance of the bar and see the staff sleeping on bar tables.

We decide to go back to town and try something else. While we are walking towards the bikes Katannal starts to poke at Minna's bum and grabs her breasts.

Minna tells him, "Do not do that! I do not like it. Please do not touch me." He does not listen and cups her breasts from behind. Minna jumps. I move quickly in front of Katannal and stop him with my left hand, braced against his right chest. I have him where I want him, face to face, with my right fist ready to go.

"*MR. KATANNAL, WHERE WE COME FROM, BOTH IN CANADA AND IN FINLAND, IT IS AGAINST THE LAW TO TOUCH A WOMAN LIKE THAT. SHE DOES NOT WANT YOU TO TOUCH HER. BE A MAN. BE A GENTLEMAN, NOT A PIG. LET ME BE CLEAR, IF YOU TOUCH MINNA AGAIN I WILL HIT YOU SO HARD YOUR TEETH WILL FLY OUT! KATANNAL, I HIT VERY HARD!*" I shout with strength and conviction with my left index finger tapping his solar plexus and right fist ready to go hard. Katannal puts his head down, says nothing, and walks with me to the bikes. The ladies and Cheera follow. The girls get on with him, Katarina separating Minna and Katannal, and take off. Cheera and I follow.

There is not a lot of room on this scooter. I have to rest my sandals on the axle bolts that stick out about an inch and a half. Cheera is not intoxicated yet he appears sleepy and does not pay attention as he steers through the darkened road.

We are driving along the main road, past a field, when I see some barricades ahead, forcing vehicles to change lanes and snake through. Cheera is not slowing down. I tap him on the shoulder and shout, "*BARRICADES AHEAD CHEERA! SLOW DOWN!*" He nods and slows down but has to use both front and back breaks to do so and almost skids out. He is not a good driver. Come on Cheera, it is a scooter you knucklehead. It does not go more that sixty kilometers an hour.

A few minutes later, I see a dark round mass on the road directly ahead of us. Cheera does not. "*LOOK OUT! LOOK OUT ON THE ROAD! DEAD WILD PIG!*" He drives right over it and we fly in the air about three feet high. He lands the bike and I fly off and roll on the ground to a scraping halt. The scrapes on my arms do not bother because there is an intense excruciating pain in my right big toe. I get up off the ground, stand up and look down. The toenail is almost torn right off. It is dangling by a thin piece of skin while blood oozes out of the nail bed.

Cheera paces in circles around his bike.

"Calm down. Take me to the tea stand up the road so that I can get some hot water and a cloth."

"Okay swami."

We meet up with the others at a small tea stand on the corner, a few blocks from the hotel. They are waiting for us there, Minna sensed that something was wrong. Minna, being a nurse, is calm when she sees me get off the bike with blood dripping from my foot. She asks for a pot of boiling water, adds some cold to it, and pours it on the toe. I pull the nail off resulting in huge throbbing pain. Minna wraps the toe with napkins. The guys drop us off at the hotel and Minna closes the gate. Katannal has the nerve to ask Minna if they can come in and party if they can get us beer. Minna says no and winks at me. She has a secret stash in the bathroom.

Minna cleans and bandages my toe. We split a couple of beers. "Thank you Minna. The throbbing pain is ebbing."

"Let's smoke one swami, it will help the pain." Minna suggests.

"I was just thinking the exact same thing. I take a joint out of my cigarette case and light it. Mary Jane takes away the sharp pain within minutes.

Katarina says, "I am very sorry that happened to you swami. I knew that we should not have gone with those guys."

Minna says, "I am also sorry swami. Thank you for giving Katannal shit. He is a pig."

"Do not feel bad Katarina or Minna. It was a freak accident. Minna, you are welcome about shutting Katannal down. I actually enjoyed witnessing the coward cower."

The pain is gone. We continue to talk outside the room, sitting on faded white plastic chairs, around an old wooden table. Katarina is leaving for home in three days while Minna is staying on to travel North India for two weeks.

"I will miss you ladies when I leave tomorrow night. Your company has been wonderful." I say.

Katarina replies, "You are a wonderful man swami. You are much fun. After you complete your book and get published you can have all of us come to Canada for a reunion."

"That is a good idea Katarina." Minna says. She adds, "We will request the book in Finland before we come and hopefully help with international sales. I am excited for you swami."

The drizzle of the shower is heard. It is a nice way to awaken, opposed to an alarm clock. The showers here are also cool and quick. It is good that the shower is cool, it helps me as I look at Minna's beautiful naked body while she towels off in front of me. I dry off, doing my best not to break the two-second rule. Niagra Falls, Niagra Falls, I think. *Sometimes, being a gentleman takes discipline and thoughts of ice cold water.* After we get dressed, we leave for breakfast.

Following a good long walk, we go back to the room and change for the beach. Minna dresses the toe and we are ready to go. Minna figures that even if the salt water gets through the plastic wrapping, it will be good for any possible infection.

"Is that a beach bar and restaurant to rest in and have a beer ladies?"

"Yes swami. Let's go in but for only one or two." Katarina answers.

Katarina and Minna fill me in on their recent travels. I tell them about Madurai, Silva, Sammy, Tariq, Kodaikanal and Gunvald staying on there.

Katarina suggests that we go to the beach. Minna and Katarina lead the way while I limp behind. The beach is large and long to the water. The wind is brisk adding to the white caps of the waves. We put our blankets down thirty feet from shore.

A group of peddlers approach us. The group of seven includes an older fellow. I ask him if he can bring us bottled water and beer. He does the head wiggle and leaves. Katarina and Minna study the bracelets and necklaces offered by an old woman and four young girls.

Walking slowly into the ocean I notice the steepness of the shore and the fast moving sand below my feet. I am over my head ten feet from where the waves break. This is not a safe place to swim, so I make it short. I stay in for ten minutes and return. "Ladies, the Bay of Bengal is harsh here. The waves move you hard and the walk in is quite steep."

Minna replies, "We do not swim here. We can feel the wind and sand blowing at us. Let's move our blankets back."

We do so and get comfortable. Sitting, facing each other, we reflect upon our time in India. It is quiet here with no other tourists on the beach. It is easy for us to contrast it with Kovalam Beach where vendors and on occasion, a tourist will get in your face. I learn more about the ladies lives in Finland and their country.

After a few hours on the beach we go back to the hotel, change and go for a late lunch. We come upon the restaurant from last night I say, "Ladies, let's stop for a moment so I can see if Katannal is here. I want to have words with him." We see him and his eyes meet mine. He looks down and away. He appears ashamed and embarrassed. That is enough for Minna and I.

The cab arrives to take me to the airport. I hug the ladies goodbye and they kiss me on each cheek. I say, "I wish I had one more day here with you ladies. You take care."

"Goodbye swami!" Katarina sings out. Minna follows with another kiss on my cheek and a discreet whisper to my ear. I get into the cab and drive away.

Sitting in an aisle seat, on the left side of the plane, is comfortable because you can lean to the right for more shoulder room. You only need to be on the lookout for hips, knocking your arm or shoulder. It is okay if a light stewardess bumps you, but not a large person. A large wandering hip can almost knock you right out of your seat. Another example of why pens go missing.

The Malaysian Airlines stewardesses are again quite friendly, professional and pretty. No male stewardesses here. Malaysian men must be confined to real man jobs. The food is fresh and the water cool. The plane is en route to Tokyo to refuel and then to Los Angles, where I will change planes for a last Delta flight into Edmonton. Big deal.

Keenan, most people think that they have a hold on the concept of time. We set our clocks, assume that they are correct, go on with our lives, despite the different calendars amongst cultures. If we think of time zones, leap years, light years, pulsars, black holes, we can begin to appreciate that time is not a constant and it is difficult to define. What actually is time? Is the future and past real? Can we use the past to predict the future? Is there time after death? Is the future finite or infinite? What the hell is the quantum theory of time anyway? We think that we can perceive reality but we cannot perceive and understand all that is real. A great friend of mine, Rob, puts it this way, "If you were able to ride a comet traveling around the earth at the speed of light, you would circumnavigate the world almost eight times in one second." Einstein's General Relativity Theory, has the speed of light at about 186,000 miles per second in a vacuum. We do not know how gravitational fields and such affect the speed of light. For our purposes Keenan, if an angel spirit, soul or The Big Bastard travels at the speed of light, we know that they can travel very, very fast.

The plane lands in Tokyo. It is frustrating to land here and not be afforded the opportunity to step out of the airport and explore the city. Perhaps if I had more time and money it could have happened. Who the hell wants to spend a month's rent on a hotel room for one night, or twenty dollars for an apple anyway?

We re-board the plane for take off. It is going to be a long overnight flight. An hour later, almost all the passengers are asleep. I cannot sleep. It is late into the morning and it is pitch black below.

The Big Bastard

It is spring and I had met Heather a few months earlier in Manzanillo, Mexico, while on a golf holiday with my best buddy, Lou, a man nicknamed Zoolander and his buddy, Fancy Boy. Heather flew from Toronto to visit me in Edmonton for two weeks. We are in love. Heather is my soul mate. *Treasure your soul mate kid as you may only be blessed with one per lifetime.*

> Asleep in the Penthouse master bedroom
> in the middle of the night.
> I wake up and raise my head and look at the half moon,
> eyes close for a few minutes and then
> the loud buzz sound
> ceiling opens up
> Big Bastard drops in!
> All thirty feet of him.
> He has not aged.
> This time, I'm not a scared little boy.

The Big Bastard and I are not in the master bedroom, nor any room. We are in a black space without walls, doors or anything. There is no ending in sight nor any beginning, just a big black nothingness space. The only thing to be seen, besides The Big Bastard and myself, is a far away star that casts a weak diffused soft and subtle ray of light. The light does not cast a shadow on our faces or on the absent floor.

The Big Bastard looks almost the same as he did a few decades ago. You would think that he would have aged some. The Big Bastard has changed in that he has stayed up with the times. He now sports a fashionable, triangular black, soul patch along with thin sideburns, that curve down his face toward his chin, ending in a small forked point. He is wearing fancy black pants and an expensive white long sleeve collared shirt. It is a very nice shirt, looks like it is a Sartoriale. His black shoes are even polished. Go figure. Fancy fashion aside, he is the same menacing muscular red skinned evil thirty foot dark eyed devil.

The Big Bastard and I stand twenty feet apart from one another. I look up at his menacing face and our eyes meet. I recall the years of torment he caused me as a child. I stare at him square in the eyes and think, "You are a bloody coward for causing me years of anguish when I was a boy."

He does not speak, yet I receive his message, "You and your dear God allowed me to torment you."

I think, "Those are fighting words you big shit of a coward." He chuckles, sneers and pumps his chest like a beefed up steroid hero in the gym. His glare is frightening. One major difference with now and thirty years ago, is that I am not a little boy in my pajamas, laying frozen on a bunk bed. I am standing up and facing The Big Bastard, wearing white boxer shorts, with my fists clenched and brow furrowed. I am standing up to The Big Bastard with my fists ready to go, thinking and knowing that it is not the size of the dog in the fight but the size of the fight in the dog that prevails.

I yell at The Big Bastard, "Get down here you loser evil bastard! Come down here and fight me like a man!"

He snorts down at me and again pumps his ripped red chest. A thought is heard, "I do not have to you little puke of a human."

What seems like an instant, life moments blast through my head with a bright silver background. I see myself sleeping at my grade three desk. Then back to the old house in Melville on sixth avenue where he came most often, my bedroom, the living room, then my tent at the lake when I was in my early teens. The memory of the multitude of encounters with The Big Bastard throughout my life fires me up even more.

I focus and realize that I am still standing, glaring at The Big Bastard. I do not feel like some rock star, just rock solid. I take myself back to my favorite rock in the hills of the Qu'appelle Valley where I prayed to God as a young boy. God be with me just now—give me strength! Suddenly, I am filled with energy, from head to toe, like when I was in the ocean feeling the impact of Dad's soul.

Next thing I know, I am as tall as The Big Bastard. We are eye to eye, with our feet on the same level for the first time. He is not any bigger than I. I outweigh him as I am not ripped like him but still strong as an ox, body fat and all. I think, you son of a bitch, you leave me alone for years then and you come to my penthouse, to my little Eden that I have dreamt about since grade nine. I thought I was done with you. He is grinning at me. I think to myself that I am going to break The Big Bastard like a wild horse. No fear at all. Positive forceful energy radiates throughout my entire body.

I skip over to The Big Bastard feet floating like Ali and stop ten feet away. He pumps his fists in the air. I quickly step forward, jabbing him with a fast left. It lands on his forehead, rocking his head back. I immediately follow with a right hook, which lands right on his ear. He stumbles a bit and I realize that he can be rocked, if not knocked out. The Big Bastard regains his balance and raises his fists. He peers behind his fists, which are the same size as mine. I almost feel like letting him give me one, just to find out how strong he is. I am crazy happy mad full of fight and am bloody loving this just now.

I spar with him, waiting patiently for an opening. He is covering his face well. I do not want to waste time and effort on a cheesy body shot; that is like playing a kings opening every time you open in chess. The Big Bastard throws a right jab at my face and I duck to the left. I jump in the air, try to bring his fists down with my left arm so I can smash his nose. It does not work, he holds his fists firm, and pushes me away. He quickly advances punching with a flurry, my arms blocking his wild punches. I defend myself using the sticky hands method. He punches out with great force right toward my chin.

The Big Bastard's right arm is thrown to the side by my left forearm block, leaving his chin open. I quickly crouch and come up with best uppercut I have ever landed. He flies ten feet in the air, landing on his back fifty yards away. I feel weightless despite having thirty-four years of anger pent up inside me. I let him get up and come at me.

The Big Bastard charges at me with his head down. I crouch, turning my right shoulder toward him, bracing for the impact. He rams me like a linebacker. We both tumble. There is no noise of falling, just the feeling of the hard impact of The Big Bastard and then rolling on nothingness. We right ourselves and face each other again. I jump up five feet and pound him with a hard right to the left side of his head. The average man's punch goes twenty miles per hour, here it seems it is more like a hundred. His head bounces back and his knees buckle. I land two more hard rights to the side of his head in quick succession, following with a swift left upper cut. He flies up, lands on his feet about nine yards away. He shakes his head and snorts loudly. His eyes bulge and the veins in his neck swell. He does not bleed. His anger builds as his face becomes glowing ember red. He may think that I am still a weakling who must kneel down and pray to God to save my little soul, however, little does The Big Bastard know is that all I care about is my son, family, mankind and being God's ass-kicker.

He charges and rams me like a locomotive. I stumble and feel a blast against the back of my head. I fly upwards in the non-air, landing fifty feet from The Big Bastard. I cannot let him charge me again. I am not good at being charged at; one needs to be really fast at moving out of the way or ducking and trip the guy as he passes. I get up and he approaches me with a steady walk. I march toward him fearlessly. We face each other with our fists raised. He jabs with his left, which is blocked by my right arm. He punches wildly with both arms and I block and block. I back up and let him go. He overextends a deep left power punch and I move my head to the right. His side is exposed so I give him a right hook to his kidney. He falters, regains his balance and turns to face me. His arms have weakened. This is my chance. I poke him on the chin with a left and follow through with a right to the bridge of his nose. His black eyes water as he stumbles backward.

The Big Bastard straightens and puts his fists up. I give him a fast right hook to the side of the head. He tries to block it but misses. Like a jack-hammer I punch him in the side of the head again and again. After the eighth pounding punch, The Big Bastard suddenly self-implodes into a burst of red and orange light, then flies off in a thin bolt of brilliant flash of red light that diminishes into nothing in less than a single second.

Keenan! The Big Bastard is gone!

I get out of bed quietly, suppressing the internal giggle of "I got you Big Bastard." I am soaking wet, so is the bed. I do not want to wake Heather. I need to let what happened sink in. My love is not ready to hear about the last visit of The Big Bastard nor am I ready to tell anyone else about it. Heather does not stir as I leave the room for the hot tub.

The sky is clear, allowing a multitude of stars to shine down on the terrace. I walk over to the railing and look down nineteen stories to the quiet street below. There is no traffic on Jasper Avenue. It must be four in the morning. It is quiet and calm. The thirty-foot stately spruce tree on the terrace does not move. The moon's reflection can be seen on the partially frozen Saskatchewan River. I fold open the hot tub lid and get in. It is hot, like it should be. I look over at Commonwealth Stadium and think of my Saskatchewan Roughriders. The snow is almost gone from the football field. Spring is close bringing new life. The tulip bulbs will soon be pushing out of the ground and preparing themselves to smile at the sun.

Looking up into the heavens, I pray to God the Creator and our Mother Nature, not mouthing a word, praying silently, thankfully … Wow! Thank you for the back up on kicking The Big Bastard's ass God! I am your man. If you ever need me for anything, I will be your huckleberry.

I sing softly over the jets in the hot tub, "I can live freely now as The Big Bastard is gone." I take a drink of my ice water and float in the hot water. *Your father is smiling so big at the moment kid, it reminds me of holding you for the first time as a newborn. Keenan, your father now fears nothing in the entire universe.*

It has been said that a person has to let The Big Bastard into oneself, otherwise he will not bother you. I do not believe that for a second. How does a four year old child <u>let</u> The Big Bastard in? Anyway, if there are any parents that have a child being tormented by The Big Bastard please give someone or this swami a call.

The Big Bastard may be gone but maybe not gone for good. I have not seen him since. I think, however, that I have seen a relative of his. Her last name reminds me of a certain pudding that contains raisins. No kidding, she could be the human equivalent of The Big Bastard's little sister. They have the same facial features. I don't miss The Big Bastard either. But if he comes back, I will kick the shit out of him again; conscious or subconscious or anything in between or beyond.

I was in Mazatlan recently with my best buddy, brother Lou, where I meet a preacher on the beach. I am building a big iguana lizard out of sand and he stops to have a look. He introduces himself as Pastor Bob. He is retired and volunteers as a Chaplain at the Calgary Airport. While I collect sand with a five-gallon pail to add more sand to the lizards back, he tells me about himself and his work. Pastor Bob is here with his wife for three weeks. He tells me about a recent change in career and his love of life. He talks while I enjoy putting the finishing touches on what Lou will call Iggy.

It is the first time that the full story of The Big Bastard is told. I am curious about what Pastor Bob thinks about the whole deal. I give him a brief history of the childhood episodes of The Big Bastard visits and then get right into it. He stops me a few times for a number of questions during the discourse regarding my belief in God, Dad's visiting soul in India and my childhood.

"That is very interesting swami. Perhaps your dad's visiting soul in India helped give you the strength to beat The Big Bastard. You do not have to worry about him coming back. You have beaten your demon young man. Good for you. Now go out and help other people beat their demons and finish your book. You have a gift of understanding God and love. You are a very spiritual person and have a lot of love to give. You are a soldier of God, act on it and get the hell away from practicing law."

"Thank you Pastor Bob. Your comments are most appreciated. What gets me, is that one would think that being a demon, representing evil and/or Satan and all, that he would do something demonic and burn me with fire balls shot out of his ass or something."

Pastor Bob asks, "Are you trying to be funny?"

I answer, "Well yes."

"Okay, let me take a picture of you and your lizard."

After he takes a couple of pictures I say to him, "That will be ten Pesos Sir."

"Where is your sign? You need a sign first before you can charge," chuckles Pastor Bob.

"Maybe we will do that another day. It will be worth a laugh." Pastor Bob leaves after I tell him to keep his eyes open for Heather and I in ten days. We do meet again.

At the end of the day son, I can only conclude once again, that religion and spirituality, no matter how much you read, no matter how far you dig, cannot fully explain the reason for man's existence and how we fit in with the universe. We do not deserve to know all the answers. Many religions attempt to provide the answers but there is no religion yet that has convinced a majority of the world's population that it has the answers and is true blue. Darwinism does not fit the bill either. Richard Dawkins and his brand of Darwinist atheism is a cop out. Atheists know not of Love. We all have much more to learn. One thing is for sure, loving your fellow man, loving your neighbor, and respecting our Creator and nature are good starting points.

What I can say about human life, within our vast universe, is that it can be course correcting in that it allows one, who loves and can think with the circular flow of time, to ride along her wave of energy. Keenan my son, catch the wave and you can see where it is taking you. Along the way mind your convictions and respect all the great Prophets for they have tried their best to show love to the world.

Thank you India, for the most suitable environment to mentally thrive in. Thank you Kavi for the opportunity to come to India in the first place and your family for the hospitality and lessons on Indian culture. I also thank all my new friends that I met in India. What a wonderful story you all contributed to.

Thank you for the tough love Dad. Thank you for all that you did for me. Your two pairs of oxford shoes work great. I have not lost a trial wearing them and no other shoes than yours are worn to court. Thanks for paying a visit after you died. Feeling your soul changed my life. I know that it is you on the cover of the book. Gunvald capturing your soul's image in the photograph is certainly A GIFT FROM THE GRAVE.

I leave you with these final thoughts, my son. This is not simply an apology for my shortcomings that elude redemption; it is a handshake, hug and a love you with my heart. My love for you is so deep, strong and pure. You are a gift from God. You are a real gift to the world and to your dad. I suspect that you are and will be all that is best in your old man.

Keenan, it does not matter whether you choose Buddha, Vishnu, Jesus, Mohammed, Creation, Darwinism, Judaism or any other world religion, or simply humanism. Be a steward for our earth and love your neighbor without being judgmental.

Go out and enjoy your life, helping as many people as you can. I will try to be around as long as I can to give you love and guidance. When your old man dies Keenan, go to a quiet place. Swim in the ocean and I will come to you. You are a wonderful, beautiful, loving, learned, and listening son. Man! I love you kid!

LET'S BRING LOVE AND JOY,
TO AND THROUGHOUT THE WORLD,
BROTHERS AND SISTERS!

978-0-595-46777-8
0-595-46777-6

Printed in the United States
109061LV00004B/142-1098/P